Wedding PAPERCRAFTS

Create Your Own Invitations, Decorations and Favors
to Personalize Your Wedding

FROM THE EDITORS
OF NORTH LIGHT BOOKS

NORTH LIGHT BOOKS
Cincinnati, Ohio
www.artistsnetwork.com

Wedding Papercrafts. Copyright © 2004 by North Light Books.
Manufactured in China. All rights reserved.
The patterns and drawings in the book are for personal use of reader.
By permission of the publisher, they may be either hand-traced
or photocopied to make single copies, but under no circumstances may
they be resold or republished. It is permissible for the purchaser to make
the projects contained herein and sell them at fairs, bazaars and craft shows.
No other part of this book may be reproduced in any form or by any electronic
or mechanical means including information storage and retrieval systems
without permission in writing from the publisher, except by a reviewer,
who may quote a brief passage in review.
Published by North Light Books, an imprint of F+W Publications, Inc.,
4700 East Galbraith Road, Cincinnati, Ohio 45236. (800) 289-0963.
First edition.

08 07 06 05 04   5 4 3 2 1

Library of Congress Cataloging-in-Publication Data
Wedding papercrafts : create your own invitations, favors and decorations
to personalize your wedding / Editors of North Light Books.
p. cm.
Includes index.
ISBN 1-55870-653-4 (alk. paper)
1. Paper work. 2. Wedding decorations. 3. Wedding stationery.
4. Weddings--Equipment and supplies. I. North Light Books (Firm)

TT870.W37 2004

745.594'l--dc22   2004043430

Designer: Leigh Ann Lentz
Layout Artist: Kathy Bergstrom
Production Coordinator: Sara Dumford
Photographers: Christine Polomsky, Tim Grondin and Al Parrish
Photography Stylist: Janet A. Nickum

METRIC CONVERSION CHART

TO CONVERT	TO	MULTIPLY BY
Inches	Centimeters	2.54
Centimeters	Inches	0.4
Feet	Centimeters	30.5
Centimeters	Feet	0.03
Yards	Meters	0.9
Meters	Yards	1.1
Sq. Inches	Sq. Centimeters	6.45
Sq. Centimeters	Sq. Inches	0.16
Sq. Feet	Sq. Meters	0.09
Sq. Meters	Sq. Feet	10.8
Sq. Yards	Sq. Meters	0.8
Sq. Meters	Sq. Yards	1.2
Pounds	Kilograms	0.45
Kilograms	Pounds	2.2
Ounces	Grams	28.4
Grams	Ounces	0.04

ABOUT THE DESIGNERS

Marie Browning

A rich family history of craftsmanship nurtured Marie at an early age, and she knew her passion for creativity would someday become her business. This vision has become a reality, as opportunities helped her create Marie Browning Creates, a design and consulting business in the craft trade. Marie has written over twelve titles in the creative living field, including *Inspired by the Garden* from North Light Books. Numerous magazine articles, project sheets for manufacturers and project instructions for virtual sites are also part of her writing career. She has also participated in product development in the craft industry. This includes helping Environmental Technologies with the AromaGel program, an innovative and award-winning gelled air freshener. Marie lives and runs her business on Vancouver Island in beautiful British Columbia. Her first love is her family: husband Scott and children Katelyn, Lena and Jonathan. Find out more about Marie at www.mariebrowning.com.

Linda Holloway

Linda Holloway is a self-taught artist who enjoys a variety of art and craft mediums. She has taught a wide range of paper art classes including cardmaking, bookbinding, paper casting, papermaking, and scrapbooking.

Linda has worked in the past as a floral designer, and she was a buyer for a paper arts store for eight years. Samples of her work have been published in *The Rubber Stamper* and in *Today's Creative Home Arts* magazines.

She lives in Minnesota with her husband, Clarion. Linda is the mother of two grown daughters and the grandmother to a wonderful grandson.

TABLE OF CONTENTS

Cheryl Ann Manning
and
Bruce Alan Lyke
request the honor
of your presence
at their marriage
on Saturday,
the twenty-fifth of October
Two thousand and three
at two in the afternoon
Jesus People Church
2400 Nicollet Avenue South
Minneapolis, Minnesota

Please join us
for the
reception following
the ceremony in
Fellowship Hall

Music from
Cheryl and Bruce's
Wedding

October 25, 2003

he favor of a reply is requested
ore October 11, 2003   regrets

INTRODUCTION

As you prepare for your wedding, you are probably exploring ways to make the celebration unique and memorable. Papercrafts are a perfect way to turn your wedding into a one-of-a-kind event, giving you the opportunity to mark the occasion with your personality and individual style.

And if the idea of creating these papercrafts to make them more personalized appeals to you, you have found the right book! Offering several theme-based projects, this book instructs you how to create not only your invitation but your very own "personal line" of coordinated wedding paper accessories. With these crafts, your special day will have a distinct look, custom made by and for you.

Whether you are an experienced papercrafter or an eager beginner, the projects on the following pages will provide valuable guidance and endless inspiration. Let the projects serve as a springboard for your creativity, and set your imagination free as you consider the many possibilities. Perhaps you would like to adopt a particular theme, honor your cultural heritage or emphasize a certain aspect of you and your betrothed. You can follow the theme-based projects "by the book," or you can mix and match the projects to accommodate your own ideas. Once you investigate the projects, you'll find how easy it is to modify each one to reflect your own taste.

Wedding papercrafts are sure to create a lasting impression on your guests. From the moment they open the wedding invitation, your guests will know that your wedding day will be special. The crafts, which range from invitations to favors to thank-you notes, will make the day something your guests look forward to, celebrate and remember. Your papercrafts will surely be treasured as beautiful mementos of an unforgettable wedding!

GETTING STARTED

In choosing to create your wedding papercrafts, you have found a unique way to personalize your special day. The projects and ideas in this book cover a variety of skill levels and time commitments, as well as a wide range of styles. Before you select the projects that you'll make for your wedding, consider the following four questions to help you narrow your choices for invitations and accessories:

- What is your skill level with papercrafts? Making your wedding invitations and accessories can be as simple or as involved as you choose. Your skill level, experience and familiarity with papercrafting should match the complexity of the projects you select.

- What is the availability of papercrafting materials in your area? Your range of papercraft designs will largely depend on your access to paper and other supplies. Art, craft and office supply stores as well as scrapbook, stamping, and stationery shops are all good sources for materials. Look at listings in your yellow pages if you are not familiar with the stores in your area, or search the Internet for materials that you can order online (see Resources on page 125).

- What is the time frame for completing your wedding papercrafts? Consider how much time you can realistically put aside to work on your paper projects. Take into account all the deadlines you face, including the dates by which you must order paper, send invitations and complete wedding favors. It is important to start the projects well in advance of these deadlines. Also consider how labor intensive your projects will be and whether or not you will have friends helping you.

- What is your budget for wedding invitations and reception papercrafts? Your budget may determine which projects and materials are feasible. Making invitations and favors yourself can save you money, or cost just as much, if not more, than ready-made items.

After considering the above questions, start thinking about the style and the design of your wedding papercrafts. The following considerations may help you formulate a more personalized design.

Theme
Is there a theme that runs through your wedding ceremony and reception? You can carry that theme over into your invitations and paper accessories.

Time of Year
During what season or time of the year will your wedding take place? You may want your papercrafts to include colors, flowers or decorations that are commonly associated with that season.

Flowers
What flowers have you selected for your wedding day? If there is a dominant flower in your arrangements, you may want to incorporate it as a design element.

Colors
Does your wedding have a color scheme? The colors and shades that you are using may provide a good basis for your papercrafts.

With the answers to these questions in mind, head to the starting point of your papercrafting journey: the invitations!

INVITATIONS & MORE

The invitation sets the stage for your wedding ceremony and reception. It provides the guests with their first glimpse into the wedding day and gives them an idea of what to expect. This section introduces different formats for invitations, gives some information about how to word your invitation, and addresses the many options for enclosures to include with the invitation. Finally, you can consider a list of other wedding decorations and accessories that you may want to match to your invitations to create a whole set of coordinated papercrafts.

INVITATION FORMATS

There are many presentation styles for wedding invitations. To get ideas, browse through wedding invitation catalogs, bridal magazines and wedding Internet sites. Following is a list of basic invitation formats. These formats can be used for all of your wedding papercrafts, from your invitations to your wedding programs to your thank-you notes. You can create your own unique design using one of these formats alone or combined with one or more other formats.

Side-Fold or Book Style

This invitation is folded in half and opens like a book. The event information can be printed on the outside cover or on the inside. An example shown in this book is the spring watercolor invitation (page 24). The snowflake invitation (page 100) is a combination of the book and layered styles.

A side-fold invitation (for complete project, see page 92)

A layered invitation (for complete project, see page 72)

Flat or Layered Invitation

This invitation generally has no folds. It is a flat piece of paper, often layered with other papers and secured in some fashion. Examples in this book include the bridal shower invitation (page 18) and the pressed daisy invitation (page 42).

A matchbook style card (for complete project, see page 25)

Top-Fold or Matchbook Style

This invitation opens up like a matchbook cover. You can fold it exactly in half, like the book style, or you can fold it so that the front panel is a bit shorter than the back panel. It could also feature a flap that catches the top panel and holds it down, just like a matchbook. An example in this book is the snowflake thank-you card (page 102). A variation of this style is used on the burgundy pocket invitation (page 62).

A trifold invitation (for complete project, see page 52)

Trifold

This invitation is folded twice to create a three-paneled surface where one fold overlaps the other. The Celtic invitation (page 52) is a fine example of this style.

A band around an invitation (for complete project, see page 62)

Band

The band, typically made from a strip of paper, is placed around the invitation. It can be secured with a piece of double-sided tape, an adhesive dot, a sticker or a wax seal. A band can hold a gatefold invitation closed or keep a wrap in place around an invitation. An example in this book is the burgundy pocket invitation (page 62).

A wrap around an invitation (for complete project, see page 32)

Wrap

This piece of paper is wrapped around the entire invitation, and it can replace the traditional inner envelope. It is usually made of thin transparent paper or handmade paper. The beaded leaf invitation (page 32) is an example of this style.

A gatefold invitation (for complete project, see page 82)

Gatefold

This invitation is folded twice to create three panels. The outside panels are folded inward to meet in the center, like French doors. The Asian invitation (page 82) in this book is an example of a gatefold card.

COMPONENTS OF AN INVITATION

At one time, customs and traditions determined the standard invitation presentation, size and wording. Many of these customs are still regarded as conventional standards today. However, in our modern and more casual social atmosphere, you are not limited to these standards. Invitation etiquette has become increasingly flexible as the choice of shapes, sizes and phrasing has broadened. Your invitation should reflect your own personal style while presenting clear information.

Following are some common components of an invitation set. Choose the elements that make sense for your unique wedding.

The Invitation

The invitation to the ceremony is considered the main and most important component of the invitation set. It provides the "who, what, where and when" of the wedding day. It may also include brief reception information.

Enclosures

The enclosures that you might include with the invitation may contain additional information about your wedding ceremony or reception.

Reception Card

Reception cards are often sent when the ceremony and reception are held at different locations and are considered two separate events. Reception cards can also be used when the guest list for the reception is larger than the list for the wedding ceremony. You might also choose to make a separate reception card if you want your guests to be aware of some particular feature to your reception, such as dancing or special entertainment, or if you want your guests to participate in some unique activity, such as sharing a poem or a story about the couple.

Direction and Map Cards

Direction and map cards are especially helpful when the wedding or reception is held in a large metro area or when many guests are traveling from out of town. Direction cards give simple but explicit directions to the wedding and reception sites. Map cards provide maps showing different routes to the locations. Check with your ceremony and reception facilities; they often have ready-made maps and/or printed directions that you can copy and include with your invitations. Usually, when direction or map cards are used, the street address is not given on the invitations. If your ceremony and reception are at different sites, you may want to make extra map cards to be distributed at the ceremony.

Response Cards and Envelopes

The response card is the primary means of determining who will attend the event. It is your way of keeping count of guests so you can plan accordingly in terms of programs, party favors, seating arrangements and food. The response cards are usually printed in the same style as the invitation. They can be flat or folded with printing on the outside, and they are accompanied by a self-addressed, stamped envelope. A less expensive alternative is to use a self-addressed, stamped postcard. The size of a response card is typically 3½" x 5" (9cm x 13cm).

Area Hotel Information

If several guests are coming from out of town, it is a good idea to provide information on accommodations that are close to the ceremony and reception locations. Include this information on the back of the direction or map card.

Inner Envelope

Ready-made invitations often include an extra envelope into which the invitation and the enclosures are inserted before being placed in the outer mailing envelope. The inner envelope is not necessary when making your own invitations. It is difficult to find an envelope that fits perfectly into a slightly larger envelope (invitation printers often design and make their own envelopes). An alternative to an inner envelope is a wrap, which can hold the invitation and the enclosures together in the outer envelope.

At-Home Card: These small cards provide the bride and groom's new home address. They can also include any change to the bride's name after the wedding as well as the expected return date from the honeymoon. They can be the size of the response card, 3½"x 5" (9cm x 13cm), or the size of a business card, 2" x 3½" (5cm x 9cm). At-home cards can be sent with the invitations, or they can be sent after the wedding.

SAVE-THE-DATE
CARDS

The save-the-date card is a way of notifying your guests of your wedding date. This is especially thoughtful if you are having out-of-town guests or if you are getting married on a holiday weekend or during the summer months, when guests might be planning vacations. These cards are not intended to replace the invitations and are usually sent out three to six months in advance, though they could be sent out as early as a year before the wedding. They are usually small cards sent in envelopes or as postcards. You can make the cards as creative and as fun as you want; it is up to you whether or not they match the invitations. Some couples send out magnets, sticky notes or picture postcards from the area where the wedding will take place, with brief wedding information printed on them. Here's an example of traditional wording for a save-the-date card:

Please hold the date of Saturday,
June twenty-fifth, two thousand and five
for the wedding of
Sandra Perkins
and
Mark Tuveson
Formal invitation to follow

WORDING THE INVITATION AND ENCLOSURES

Your invitation should contain all the information your guests need to know about the wedding: the names of the bride and groom, the date, the time(s) and the location(s). This information should be presented in a clear and understandable fashion; be sure to use the correct spelling of names and correct addresses of the ceremony and reception sites.

There are many traditional "rules" for wording your invitations. Generally speaking, the more formal your wedding, the closer you should follow these rules. Because your handmade invitations will be unique, you may not feel obliged to follow convention. However, you still might be interested in following some traditional standards.

The following is a list of formal invitation etiquette:

- With the exception of Mr. and Mrs., everything is spelled out, including the word and. Abbreviations are not used for anything else.

- The British words honour ("honour of your presence") and favour ("the favour of a reply") are used instead of their American counterparts.

- The phrase "honour of your presence" is used on invitations to ceremonies to be held in a church or other house of worship. The phrase "pleasure of your company" is used on invitations to other ceremonies and to wedding receptions.

- Names are written in full using first, middle and last. Never use nicknames, and never use initials.

- Family order is spelled out (e.g., "Senior") or indicated by Roman numerals (e.g., "III").

- Days, dates and times are spelled out.

- The year does not need to be included on the invitations. However, when the year is included, it is spelled out.

You have a wide range of options for invitation wording; on the following page are but a few examples to help you out. For more examples of wording, look in wedding invitation catalogs or on Internet sites that sell wedding invitations.

Bride's parents announcing

Mr. and Mrs. Thomas Dale Perkins
request the honour of your presence
at the marriage of their daughter
Sandra Kaye
to
Mark William Tuveson
on Saturday, the eighteenth of June,
two thousand and five
at four o'clock in the afternoon
Saint John's Lutheran Church
4842 Nicollet Avenue South
Minneapolis, Minnesota

Bride's and groom's parents announcing

Mr. and Mrs. Thomas Dale Perkins
and
Mr. and Mrs. Matthew Steven Tuveson
request the honour of your presence

Bride and groom announcing

Sandra Kaye Perkins
and
Mark William Tuveson
invite you to share in our joy
as we exchange wedding vows

Bride and groom and parents announcing

Together with their parents
Sandra Kaye Perkins
and
Mark William Tuveson
request the honour of your presence

If the reception site is the same as the wedding site and you do not want a separate enclosure for the reception information, you can simply add the information at the end of the invitation:

Mr. and Mrs. Thomas Dale Perkins
request the honour of your presence
at the marriage of their daughter
Sandra Kaye
to
Mark William Tuveson
on Saturday, the eighteenth of June,
two thousand and five
at four o'clock in the afternoon
Saint John's Lutheran Church
4842 Nicollet Avenue South
Minneapolis, Minnesota
A dessert reception will
follow the ceremony

If you want a separate card for the reception

Dinner Reception
to be held following the ceremony
at the Radisson Hotel
3656 Nicollet Avenue South
Minneapolis, Minnesota

or

Join us for dinner and dancing
at six o'clock in the evening
Radisson Hotel
3656 Nicollet Avenue South
Minneapolis, Minnesota

A more formal and traditional response card would read as follows:

The favour of a reply is requested before
the seventeenth of March
M _____
will _____ attend

If you are sending response cards

Please respond on or before
May 30, 2005
Name _____
_____ able to attend
_____ unable to attend

or

The favor of a reply is requested
on or before May 30, 2005
Name _____
____ Baked Chicken
____ Roast Beef
____ Vegetarian Entrée

The guest fills in the first line with the name(s), using M as the initial letter for the title (example: "Mr. and Mrs. Robert Smith"). The second line is left blank to indicate the intention to attend, or the guest writes the word "not" to indicate inability to attend. Because some people may not be familiar with the traditional use of M it may be clearer to use "Name."

Sometimes people forget to write their names on the response cards. If you want to make sure you know who returned the response cards, you can place a small, inconspicuous number on the back of each response card and compile a list to record the guests' names with their numbers. Your list will tell you who sent a card if the guest forgets to.

INVITATION EXTRAS

Here are a few tidbits to help you send out your invitation with success:

- Make more invitations than you think you may need. You'll want some on hand for last minute additions and one or more for keepsakes.

- Order a few extra outer envelopes in case of addressing errors.

- Double check your zip codes. The United States Postal Service makes it easy to verify any postal code you may have a question about at their website, **www.usps.gov.**

- Take a completed invitation to the post office and have it weighed to be sure you have the correct postage.

- Remember to include a stamp on the response card's envelope or postcard.

- Prepare two separate guest lists. A "mandatory" list for those people you know you must invite, and a "secondary" list for people you'd like to invite if you can accommodate them. Mail out invitations to those on your "mandatory" list a little early, then if you start receiving regrets, you can begin sending invitations to those on your "secondary" list.

ASSEMBLING THE INVITATION

When you assemble the invitation package, insert the invitation so that its front faces the back flap of the outside envelope. If you use an inner envelope, leave it unsealed. When your guests open the envelope and pull out the invitation, they will find the text face up, ready to read. If you use a wrap, insert the invitation so that any text on the wrap will be readable to a right-handed person pulling it out of the envelope.

If you include enclosures with your invitation, place them behind the main invitation and printed side up. This allows the guest to see the invitation first, followed by the other informational pieces. Enclosures should be placed in the following order under the invitation: reception card; response card (tucked under the flap of, not inserted into, its accompanying envelope); any additional enclosures, such as maps, directions or at-home cards.

ADDRESSING THE ENVELOPES

The envelope serves not only to hold all your invitation elements but also as the place where you communicate who exactly you're inviting to the wedding. Where and how you write this information depends on whether you're including an inner envelope.

If you do use an inner envelope, address the outer envelope to the person or the couple you're inviting.

On the inner envelope, follow these guidelines to write who is invited:

- Traditionally, only the title(s) and surname of the invited guests ("Mr. and Mrs. Johnson") should be written on the inner envelope.

- Write below the parents' names the first names of any children that are invited. If more than one child is invited, write the names starting with the oldest and proceeding in order to the youngest. If the children are not invited, omit their names.

- If the invitation is being sent to a single guest and you would like to extend the invitation to an unknown escort, address the inner envelope with your friend's name followed by "and guest".

If you do not include an inner envelope, you need to write all guest information on the outer envelope. If you are inviting a single person, address it to the person or to the person "and guest". For a family, address the envelope to the members that are invited (e.g., "Mr. and Mrs. Luke Johnson, Emil, Ryan, and Gail"). If the entire family is invited, address it to the person or couple "and family". Be sure to include a return address on the outer envelope in case a guest's address is incorrect.

WHEN TO SEND

Plan to send your invitations out four to six weeks before the wedding date to allow time for your guests to make plans and to respond. If you are inviting many out-of-town guests, send your invitations out eight or more weeks in advance.

COORDINATING PIECES

As you design your wedding invitations, consider how you would like your corresponding paper accessories to complement the invitation set. You can make your invitation design carry all the way through to the thank-you note, or you can choose only certain elements of the design, such as the paper or the theme, to create a common thread. (If you decide to use the same paper, remember that you can save time and sometimes money by buying the supplies for all your wedding stationery pieces at once.)

A table card (for complete project, see page 35)

Program
The program provides an overview of the ceremony. It often lists the members of the wedding party and breaks down the ceremony into chronological events. The program can also include verses, prayers, a message from the couple or descriptions of customs used in the ceremony.

Table Cards
Table cards are used for assigned seating at the reception. The cards show the number of each table. Escort cards are used in conjunction with the table cards. An escort card bears the name of a guest with the guest's table number. They are typically placed at the reception entrance, where guests will find them immediately.

Menu Card
Though generally used for formal sit-down receptions, menu cards can also be used for receptions with a buffet-style meal. The menu simply lists the items to be served, sometimes with a brief description of the courses or buffet options.

Thank-You Card
Thank-you notes are written to express gratitude for your guests' gifts and for their attendance. A thank-you note is usually the size of a small note card. Traditionally, a 8½" x 5½" (22cm x 14cm) piece of card stock, folded in half to measure 4¼" x 5½" (11cm x 14cm), is used as the thank-you stationery and sent in a size A-2 envelope.

You can save money by sending thank-you postcards, which require less paper, less postage and no envelopes. Feel free to be creative with the postcard design. The front of the card could include a photo from your wedding, color copied or computer printed, which would serve as a nice keepsake for your guests.

A wedding program (for complete project, see page 54)

A menu card (for complete project, see page 95)

All sorts of other creative ideas for invitations and much, much more are included in the sections that follow. Let your imagination soar as you begin to plan your wedding papercrafts!

a whisper of ROMANCE

Before the festivities of the wedding, you get to experience the fun and friendship of the bridal shower. The contemporary design of this set will leave no doubt that "love" is the theme of the party! Because love and romance are never out of season, this theme is versatile — you can use this set of projects any time of the year!

The soft colors, fancy curlicues, and cheerful font promise a lighthearted atmosphere for an intimate gathering of friends. You will be proud to send out your invitations and even prouder to show off your coordinated decorations and favors, all bearing pretty pink hearts.

Simple cutout hearts provide unique table décor, and a beautiful gift candle honors the bride. Send your guests home with a special heart-shaped box—you decide what to put inside! Prepare to delight your guests with these charming pink and silver papercrafts.

INVITATION • CANDLE FAVOR • HEART FAVOR BOX • TABLE CONFETTI

INVITATION

Shake things up with a little fun and frivolity! In soft pink and metallic silver,
the swirls and curls of this invitation will make your bridal shower irresistible!

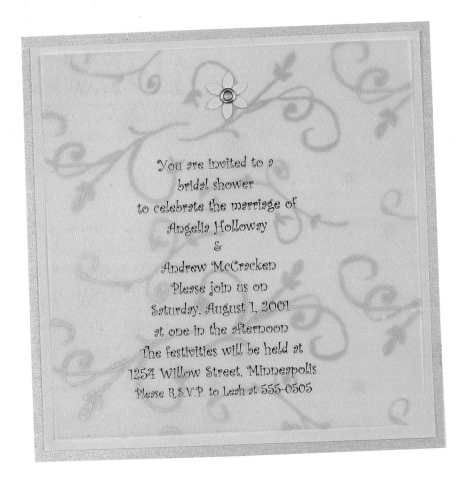

You are invited to a
bridal shower
to celebrate the marriage of
Angelia Holloway
&
Andrew McCracken
Please join us on
Saturday, August 1, 2001
at one in the afternoon
The festivities will be held at
1254 Willow Street, Minneapolis
Please R.S.V.P. to Leah at 555-0505

what you will need

- 8½" × 11" (22cm × 28cm) pink flower translucent paper
- 8½" × 11" (22cm × 28cm) silver metallic cardstock
- 8½" × 11" (22cm × 28cm) pink cardstock
- 5½" (14cm) square envelope
- ⅛" (3mm) silver eyelet
- scissors
- ruler
- pencil
- daisy punch
- ⅛" (3mm) hole punch
- eyelet setter
- hammer
- cutting mat
- double-sided tape

1 Create a document for pieces that are 4¾" (12cm) square. Center the text and begin the words 1" (3cm) down from the top of the paper. Here, the font Curlz MT bold is used at 14pt, with the last line being 12pt. Print the wording onto the translucent paper. Trim the paper to 4¾" (12cm) square. (See Printing on Your Computer, page 110.)

2 Cut the pink cardstock to a 5" (13cm) square, and cut the metallic paper to a 5¼" (13.5cm) square.

3 Using the scraps from the pink cardstock, punch out a small daisy with the daisy punch. Then carefully punch a hole in the center of the daisy with the ⅛" (3mm) hole punch.

4 To assemble the invitation, adhere the pink cardstock square in the center of the silver cardstock square with double-sided tape. Center the printed vellum on top of the pink cardstock. Measure ⅞" (2cm) down from the top of the invitation, then make a mark in the center of the card with a pencil. Punch a hole, through the three papers, with the ⅛" (3mm) punch.

5 Place the punched pink daisy over the hole in the papers and line up the holes. Place the silver eyelet in the hole and set it. (See Setting Eyelets, page 118.) Mail the invitation in the square envelope.

TIP

Make a punch template if you are punching a lot of invitations so you won't have to measure every invitation. Take a 5¼" (13cm) square of cardstock and punch an ⅛" (3mm) hole ⅞" (2cm) down from the top of the piece of paper, in the center of the paper width. Just place this template over the three stacked papers and punch in the template's hole.

CANDLE FAVOR

This personalized candle favor celebrates the honored couple by featuring the names of the bride and groom and the wedding date. Attached to the silver raffia is a "love" charm, accenting the romantic theme of the shower.

FAVOR IDEAS

Candles are just one of many wonderful favor ideas for either the shower or the wedding. Let your guests know how much you appreciate them with one of these special favors:

- heart-shaped sugar cookies
- wrapped chocolates, such as handmade truffles
- candied almonds, also known as Jordan almonds
- flower seeds
- flower bulb in cellophane bag
- small framed photo of the bride and groom
- small jars of honey or jam
- bath salts
- lottery tickets
- package of hot chocolate

what you will need

- pink pillar candle, 3" (8cm) tall and 3" (8cm) in diameter
- 12" (30cm) square white paper with silver design
- 20" (51cm) silver raffia or cord
- silver "love" charm on "O" ring
- scissors
- ruler
- pencil
- double-sided tape

1 Create a document for 2" × 10" (5cm × 25cm) strip. Start the text ½" (1cm) down from the top of the paper. Here, the font Gigi was used at 16pt. Print the wording on the white paper. Trim the printed band to 2" × 10" (5cm x 25cm).

2 Wrap the band around the candle. On one end of the band place a small strip of double-sided tape. Fasten the other end of the band onto the tape. Make sure the band is snug on the candle.

3 Wrap the piece of raffia or cord around the candle twice with the ends positioned in the front of the candle. Slip the charm on one of the ends and tie the two ends in a knot.

HEART BOX FAVOR

This cute and easy heart box holds whatever favor you'd like to surprise your guests with. With the versatility of the heart motif, you can use this box for practically any wedding-related event—even for the wedding itself!

what you will need

- 4" × 7" (10cm × 18cm) piece of matboard
- 8½" x 11" (22cm × 28cm) pink mulberry paper
- 8½" × 11" (22cm × 28cm) pink cardstock
- 8½" × 11" (22cm × 28cm) white embossed translucent paper
- 8½" × 11" (22cm × 28cm) silver paper
- 20" (51cm) of silver cord
- 10" (25cm) of ¼" (6mm) wide silver wired ribbon
- silver heart charm
- scissors
- pencil
- bone folder
- glue stick
- glue gun
- heart pattern (on page 122)

1 Cut two 3¼" (8cm) squares and two 1½" (4cm) squares from the silver paper. Use these pieces to construct the silver box following the quick box instructions on page 114. Set aside.

2 To cut the matboard into two 3" (8cm) heart shapes, use the bone folder and heart pattern to score the shapes, then use scissors to cut all the way through the board. Cut two 4" (10cm) squares from the mulberry paper. Use the glue stick to glue the mulberry paper to the matboard with the white side of the board facing the paper. Trim the paper ¼" (6mm) larger than the heart shape, and fold and glue the edges over to cover the matboard shape. Repeat with the second heart.

3 With the glue gun, glue the silver cord around the edges of both hearts.

4 With the scissors and heart pattern, cut out two 3" (8cm) hearts from the pink cardstock and two 3" (8cm) hearts from the white embossed vellum paper. Glue the vellum hearts onto the pink mulberry hearts for the lid and the pink paper hearts onto the bottom of the hearts.

5 Glue the box bottom to the top of one of the heart shapes. Place the lid on the box and then glue the top heart on it, making sure the heart shapes line up.

6 To finish the box, glue on a silver wired ribbon shoestring bow (see Shoestring Bow, page 120) and add the silver charm to the top of the heart using the glue gun.

TABLE CONFETTI

*This charming confetti is the perfect shower decoration —
simple, original and sure to impress. Scattered across
a table or hung from the ceiling, these hearts can be
displayed creatively to generate a festive atmosphere!*

SHAPE CUTTING TOOL

Cutting out these hearts would be a
perfect job for a shape-cutting tool.
These personal die-cut systems
provide a new way to cut your own
professional-looking paper shapes.
The system is very user-friendly, and
the shape templates are available in a
wide selection of motifs, letters,
numbers, packages and envelopes. The
tool itself has a circular handle with a
cutting blade underneath. To use it,
place your paper and plastic template
on a cutting mat, then follow the edge
of the template with the cutting tool.

what you will need

- rose-printed vellum
- white vellum
- silver paint pen
- craft knife
- cutting mat
- decorative-edge scissors
- heart pattern (on page 122)

1 With the silver paint pen, write *Love* all
over the white vellum. Then use the craft knife
and cutting mat to cut lots of hearts from the
papers, using the heart pattern.

2 Cut around the negative shapes left in the
paper with the decorative-edge scissors to
create the heart-shaped rings.

Rise up, my love, my fair one.
And come away
For lo, the winter is past,
The rain is over and gone.
The flowers appear on the earth;
The time of singing has come...
Song of Solomon 2:10.12

Douglas and Trish
July 14, 2001

the innocence of SPRING

Springtime is a season of new life, the ideal time for a bride and groom to celebrate their new life together as husband and wife. A perfect choice for an April or May wedding, this theme draws its inspiration from lilies of the valley, violets and other flowers that bloom during the spring months. To accentuate the theme, include some or all of these blossoms in your floral arrangements.

The combination of rubber stamps and watercolor markers gives each object a one-of-a-kind, hand-drawn appearance. Though the stamps differ, their consistent style is the unifying factor between the invitation, the wedding program, the gift book, the table card and the thank-you card. Your guests will revel in the springtime charm of each lovely project!

INVITATION · THANK-YOU CARD · PHOTO BOOKLET GIFT · TABLE CARD · COLUMN TWIST FAVOR

INVITATION

Soft colors and the hand-drawn look of the rubber stamp design give this invitation the artistic charm of an original watercolor. With the wide selection of rubber stamps available today, you are sure to find several springtime flowers from which to choose!

Rise up, my love, my fair one.
And come away
For lo, the winter is past,
The rain is over and gone.
The flowers appear on the earth;
The time of singing has come...
Song of Solomon 2:10-12

- 8½" × 11" (22cm x 28cm) white deckle-edge cardstock, 2 sheets
- A-7 envelope
- dark gray dye-ink pad
- large lily-of-the-valley rubber stamp (Printworks)
- small lily-of-the-valley rubber stamp (Printworks)
- spring flowers rubber stamp (Printworks)
- watercolor markers: ivory, dark green and yellow
- paintbrush
- plastic wrap or foam plate
- scissors
- ruler
- pencil
- bone folder

The most joyous of occasions
is the union of man and wife
in celebration of life
Trish Lynn Pindor
and
Douglas Gene Johnson
invite you to join them in asking
God's blessing upon this holy union
on Saturday, the fourteenth of July
two thousand and one
at five o'clock in the evening
Saint Edward's Church
9401 Nesbitt Avenue South
Minneapolis, Minnesota

1 Create a document for a 10" × 7" (25cm × 18cm) card folded in half to 5" × 7" (13cm × 18cm). Start the wording for the front of the card 4" (10cm) from the top of the card, centering the text. Start the wording for the inside of the card 1¼" (3cm) from the top and center it as well. Here, the Venezia-Light font was used at 16pt on the outside and at 18pt on the inside. Print the front and inside wording of the invitation. As you print, be sure that the deckle edge of the paper is on the front of the invitation. After printing, trim the card to 10" × 7" (25cm × 18cm), then score and fold the piece in half with the bone folder.

2 Create a document for a 4" × 6" (10cm × 15cm) card. Start the text 3½" (9cm) from the top of the page, centering the text. Again the font is 18pt. Print the reception card. Trim the card to size.

3 Ink the large lily-of-the-valley rubber stamp, and stamp the cover of the invitation, centering the stamp between the top of the card and the wording. Stamp the reception card with the spring flowers rubber stamp, again centering the image. Let dry.

4 To color the stamped images, scribble on a piece of plastic wrap with the green marker. Add a little water to the colored area with the paintbrush. Test the color on a scrap piece of the invitation paper, adding more water if the color is too dark or scribbling more if it's too light. When the color is right, paint the leaves and green parts of the flowers with the brush. Do not paint the entire surface of the different areas. It will have more of a watercolored look if it is not totally covered. Repeat the process with the ivory marker for the lily-of-the-valley flowers and the yellow marker for the spring flowers. Stamp and paint the envelope as well using the small lily-of-the-valley stamp. The invitation fits a size A-7 envelope.

Dinner Reception
to be held following
the ceremony
Lakeshore country club
8800 Vincent Avenue South
Bloomington

Thank you

THANK-YOU CARD

This thank-you card introduces a new spring flower but has the same look as the other stamps used in the set. To make this card, create a document that is 5½" × 8½" (14cm × 22cm). Start the printing 7¼" (18cm) from the top of the paper. The font used here is Venezia-Light at 26pt. Use the bone folder and ruler to score and fold the card in half so that it opens horizontally. Ink and stamp the violets rubber stamp (from Printworks) onto the front of the card. Color the image with dark green and purple watercolor markers. The card fits into an A-2 envelope.

PHOTO BOOKLET GIFT

Make this booklet as a gift for each member of your wedding party, and then make one as a gift to yourself! Filled with photographs from the wedding day, it will be a lasting tribute to the beginning of your new life together.

Douglas and Trish
July 14, 2001

- 8½" × 11" (22cm × 28cm) white deckle-edge cardstock, 4 sheets
- 20" (51cm) of ⅛" (3mm) ivory
- double-faced satin ribbon
- dark gray dye-ink pad
- small lily-of-the-valley rubber stamp (Printworks)

- watercolor markers: ivory and dark green
- paintbrush
- plastic wrap or foam plate
- ⅛" (3mm) hole punch
- scissors
- ruler

- pencil
- bone folder
- large needle
- two small binder clips
- white craft glue

TIP

If you plan to make multiple booklets, create a master template for the holes from a heavy, colored piece of cardstock. Cut the paper to the size of the booklet and punch the holes in this paper. Then align the papers for the book with the template and punch holes where shown.

1 Create a document for a 5½" × 8½" (14cm × 22cm) cover. Begin the wording 3½" (9cm) from the top of the paper and center the text. Here, the Venezia-Light font was used at 16pt. When printing the cover, make sure the deckle edge of the paper is to the right of the text. Trim to 5½" × 8½" (14cm × 22cm).

2 Ink and stamp the small lily-of-the-valley stamp on the cover, centering it between the top of the paper and the text. Scribble on the plastic wrap with the watercolor markers, then add a bit of water. Use a paintbrush to paint parts of the flower with green and ivory as described in step 4 on page 25.

3 Cut all the full sheets of cardstock to 5½" × 8½" (14cm × 22cm). Create a template with one sheet of paper, and measure and mark with a ruler and pencil where the holes will be punched. First measure ¾" (19mm) in from the left side; all the holes will be punched along this margin. Then measure and mark 1" (3cm) from the top of the paper, 2" (5cm) from the top, 3½" (9cm) from the top and 4½" (11cm) from the top.

4 Punch holes at each of the four pencil marks. Using the punched paper as a template, punch two to three sheets of the book paper at a time until all eight sheets are done. Make sure that the printed and stamped cover is facing up when you punch it.

5 Stack the pages between the covers so that the holes line up. To hold the pages in place while you bind them, place a small clip a little to the right of the hole on the top, and place another clip by the hole at the bottom.

6 Thread one end of the ribbon through the eye of the needle so you have a 2" (5cm) to 3" (8cm) tail, (just enough for you to hold the ribbon in the needle).

7 Starting at the front of the booklet, put the needle through the top hole. Pull the needle through the hole, and leave a 4" (10cm) tail at the front of the booklet.

8 Loop the ribbon around the spine of the booklet and push the needle through the second hole, from the front of the book to the back. Pull the ribbon taut and keep it flat.

9 Loop the ribbon around the spine of the booklet and push the needle through the third hole from the front of the book to the back. Again pull the ribbon taut and make sure it is flat. Repeat for the fourth hole. Your ribbon should look like it is spiraling down around the spine to the bottom of the booklet.

10 Spiral the ribbon back up the spine, starting at the fourth hole, going around the spine and up through the third hole. Pull the ribbon taut and make sure the ribbon is flat. Loop the ribbon around the spine and pull the needle through the second hole from the back of the book to the front. Again pull the ribbon taut and make sure it is flat. Repeat from the second hole up through the first.

11 With both tail ends coming out of the front of the top hole, tie a knot with the two ends. If you like, tie a shoestring bow (see Shoestring Bow, page 120), then trim the ends of the ribbon so they are even. Add a drop of glue to the knot to hold it tied.

12 Use the bone folder and ruler to score a line slightly to the right of the holes on the front cover. This will allow the cover to open easily and will avoid an unwanted crease.

SO MANY RUBBER STAMPS

Rubber-stamping has grown into a beautiful art form with many wonderful techniques. The range of motifs available in rubber stamps is huge. Whatever motif or theme you are looking for, there will be a stamp available! You can purchase a stamp and use it for the invitations, thank-you cards, favors and even the paper napkins. Choose your stamp well, as it will be the emblem for your wedding. You can also have a rubber stamp custom made, or you can carve your own. Stamps are available in tiny sizes that can be repeated for a design, and in large sizes for instant coverage.

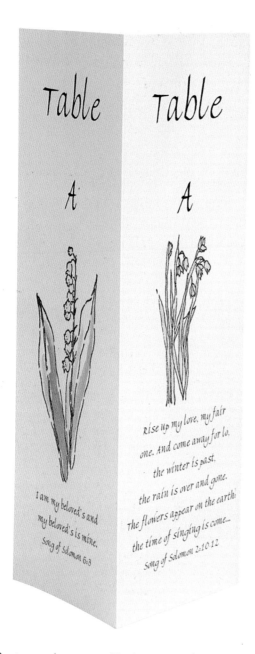

TABLE CARD

Your guests will immediately recognize the spring floral motif when they see these beautiful table cards, bearing the lily-of-the-valley stamp. This sample features a popular verse from the Song of Solomon, but you can use any verse or quote that has special meaning to you.

what you will need

- 8½" × 11" (22cm × 28cm) white cardstock
- dark gray dye-ink pad
- large lily-of-the-valley rubber stamp (Printworks)
- violets rubber stamp (Printworks)
- spring flowers rubber stamp (Printworks)
- watercolor markers: ivory, dark green, yellow and purple
- paintbrush
- plastic wrap or foam plate
- ruler
- pencil
- bone folder
- double-sided tape

1 Create a document with landscape orientation and four columns. The width of the first column (the tab to hold the card in the triangular shape) is ½" (1cm); the remaining three columns are each 3½" (9cm). Add the text ⅞" (2cm) from the top of the paper on each of the three columns. The placement of additional text will depend on the length. Here the verses start 7" (18cm), 5½" (14cm) or 4⅝" (12cm) from the top of the paper. Remember to allow enough space for the stamped image. Print the wording on the cardstock. The font used here is Venezia-Light at 72pt and 18pt The verses used are from Song of Solomon 6:3, 2:10–12 and 8:6–7.

2 Measure and mark the columns using the measurements above. With the ruler and the bone folder, score and fold the three fold lines.
3 Ink each of the stamps and stamp one on each of the three wide panels. Use the larger stamps on panels with less text and the smaller stamps on panels with more text. Center the stamps between the areas of text.
4 Scribble on the plastic wrap with the watercolor markers. Add water to the scribbling, then use a paintbrush to paint the stamped flowers. Use dark green on all the stems and leaves, ivory on the lily-of-the-valley, yellow on the spring flowers, and

purple on the violets. (See step 4 on page 25 for more thorough instructions.) Let dry.
5 Run a strip of double-sided tape down the tab on the side of the paper with the printing on it. Stick the tab onto the back of the right edge of the paper, making a triangular shape. If you must transport the table cards to the reception, use double-sided tape with a removable backing. Transport the cards flat with the tape in place on the tab, then remove the backing at the reception area and assemble the table cards.

COLUMN TWIST FAVOR

Don't be fooled by the fancy appearance of this charming little container, so perfect for holding candy favors or Jordan almonds. It is surprisingly simple to make, and it's easy to adjust if you'd like to try different sizes or shape variations.

what you will need

- 8½" × 11" (22cm × 28cm) green vellum
- 8½" × 11" (22cm × 28cm) pink vellum
- 8½" × 11" (22cm × 28cm) white text-weight paper
- 5" (13cm) of ⅛" (3mm) ivory double-faced satin ribbon
- dark gray dye-ink pad
- violets rubber stamp (Printworks)
- small lily-of-the-valley rubber stamp (Printworks)
- watercolor markers: yellow, dark green, pink
- paintbrush
- plastic wrap or foam plate
- scissors
- ruler
- pencil
- bone folder
- ⅛" (3mm) hole punch
- deckle-edged scissors
- stapler
- large needle
- double-sided tape
- glue stick

1 Cut the green vellum to 5½" × 4¼" (14cm × 11cm). Place a piece of double-sided tape along the edge of one long side and roll the piece into a cylinder, covering the width of the tape with the other long side. Press together to adhere well.

2 Pinch the bottom edge of the cylinder together, with the taped seam in the center and staple to hold.

3 Cut two strips of pink vellum to 2½" × ½" (6cm × 1cm). Score down the center of each strip lengthwise. Fold the strips in half at the scored lines, then trim the edges with the deckle-edged scissors. Glue one strip over the bottom of the pouch to hide the staples, trim excess with scissors, if necessary, and set aside the second strip.

4 Fill the pouch with the desired contents, then pinch the top edges together at a perpendicular angle to the bottom edge. Staple to hold, then glue on the second pink strip to hide the staples.

5 Punch two holes about ⅜" (1cm) apart at the top of the pouch. Take care not to punch through a staple. Using the needle, thread the ribbon through the holes and tie with a shoestring bow (see Shoestring Bow, page 120). Trim the ends.

6 Choose a floral stamp, and stamp one image onto the white paper. Color the image in with the markers and the paintbrush, as was done in step 4 on page 25. Let dry. Trim around the image with the deckle-edged scissors and glue it to the front of the pouch. If you can't find a stamp small enough for this favor, reduce a stamped image on a photocopier, then color it in with watercolor markers and trim as directed.

TIP

To add a bit of variety to any of your wedding papercrafts, create alternate versions of any element using similar techniques and materials. For these pouches, reverse the color combination and alter the floral images.

Music from
Marian and James'
Wedding
June 21, 2203

Two hearts joined as one

June 21, 2003

Marian Faith Francis
and
James Love

beaded BEAUTY

The smallest of details can make even the simplest of things very special. With swirls, curlicues, beads and felt, you can turn the ordinary green leaf into an extraordinary wedding motif. Ornamental accents make each individual leaf—and the wedding itself—an exquisite work of art!

The green leaf theme can be used for any number of reasons: Perhaps the wedding will be held outdoors during the spring or summer, perhaps the bride and groom are nature lovers, or perhaps the couple just likes the contemporary flavor of these papercraft projects. But one thing is certain—the wedding will be a singular event with an original style all its own.

You can easily adapt the color or decorative elements to give the leaf motif your own unique touch. The guests will marvel at your creativity as they enjoy the table card, pouch favors and compact disc holder. Your own blessings and wishes booklet, signed by wedding guests, will be a source of joy for years to come.

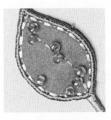

INVITATION • CD KEEPSAKE • TABLE CARD • BLESSINGS & WISHES BOOKLET • BEADED POUCH FAVOR

INVITATION

Beads and felt are a novel way to give your wedding invitation an artsy, modern feeling. Amplify this feeling by using a fancy spiral clip to attach any other invitation components!

Two hearts joined as one

June 21, 2003

Marian Faith Francis
and
James Love

This day our hearts
are joined as one.
Share with us this new beginning
the first day of our life together
on Saturday,
the twenty-first of June
Two thousand and three
at two in the afternoon
Church of the Nazarene
1214 7th Street
International Falls, Minnesota
Reception
following the ceremony
in the Blue Room

what you will need

- 12" (30cm) square green curlicue duplex paper, 2 sheets
- 8½" × 11" (22cm × 28cm) lime green cardstock
- no. 10 envelope
- felt leaf with beads (Marcel Schurman Do-Jiggies)
- 18½" (47cm) of olive raffia
- scissors
- ruler
- bone folder
- wrap template (on page 122)

1 Create a document for a 3¾" × 9" (10cm × 23cm) piece. Center the wording on the invitation, starting the words 2⅜" (6cm) down from the top; start the bottom names 1" (3cm) from the bottom of the invitation. Here the Gigi font was used at 16pt. Print the wording on the cardstock, and trim the cards to 3¾" × 9" (10cm × 23cm).

2 Cut the wrap out of the curlicue paper using the template. Score and fold the sides on the wrap, as shown on the template. The light side of the paper should be on the inside of the wrap.

3 Place the invitation inside the wrap. With the wrap closed, place the beaded leaf on the top center of the invitation. After you have determined where it should be placed, take the paper off the foam sticker on the back of the leaf and stick in place.

4 Cut one sheet of the green curlicue paper to 8½" × 11" (22cm × 28cm). Create an 8½" × 2½" (22cm × 6cm) document for the band. Leave approximately 1" (3cm) between the two lines of text (to allow for the raffia). Print the band on the light side of the curlicue paper. Here the font size is 18pt.

5 Place the band around the invitation. Fold the band around the sides of the invitation. Make sure it fits snugly and that the two back sections of the band are going straight across the back of the invitation.

6 Place the raffia around the invitation, and tie a bow in the front. Trim the ends if necessary. This invitation fits into a no.10 envelope.

Variation Idea

This alternative uses bright gold paper and includes a beautiful hand-dyed ribbon with a beaded charm created by you. Create a document for 3¾" × 9" (10cm × 23cm) cards, and print the invitation on yellow cardstock. Start the first section of words about ⅝" (2cm) from the top of the paper. Start the text of the invitation 2⅜" (6cm) from the top, and start the bottom names 1" (3cm) from the bottom of the invitation. Use the wrap template on page 122 to create the wrap. Place two or more coordinating beads on a gold jewelry pin with a head. With needle-nose pliers bend the end of wire down to create a closed loop. Cut an 18½" (47cm) length of yellow ribbon and place it around the invitation. Tie the first part of a shoestring bow in the front of the invitation (see Shoestring Bow, page 120). Slip the loop of the beaded wire onto one of the ribbon ends and finish tying the bow.

CD KEEPSAKE

The same papers and beaded felt leaf used in the invitation are used to create this pretty CD holder. Use music from the wedding or some of the bride and groom's favorite songs to create a CD. Give the CDs as wedding favors or as gifts to the people in your wedding party.

1 Cut the green curlicue paper to 8½" × 11" (22cm × 28cm). Create a document for a 3½" (9cm) square. Start the text 2⅞" (7cm) from the top of the paper. Here the Gigi font was used at 20pt. Print the label of the CD holder on the green curlicue paper. Trim the labels to size.

2 Cut the cardstock using the CD holder template. With the bone folder, score and fold the lines shown on the template.

3 Fold the two side tabs of the holder in and place double-sided tape on the tabs. Fold up the back of the CD holder onto the two tabs. Make sure everything lines up and is straight before pressing the back firmly into place.

4 Center the label on the front of the CD holder and adhere it with double-sided tape.

5 Cut a 1½" (4cm) square out of the scrap cardstock. Use double-sided tape to affix the square to the upper part of the label. Make sure the square is centered between the top of the label and the wording.

6 Take the backing off the felt leaf sticker. Stick the leaf in the center of the 1½" (4cm) square. If you want the back top flap to close, use a small hook and loop fastener to hold the flap down.

TIP

Instead of purchasing beaded embellishments like the leaf used here, you can make them yourself (see Making a Beaded Accent, page 38, for more information.)

TABLE CARD

Make the seating of your guests an easy task with these triangular prism table cards. The cards have a simple, understated look, but they are easily dressed up by adding verses, quotes or designs to the sides.

1 Cut the green curlicue paper to 8½" × 11" (22cm × 28cm).

2 Create a landscape document with four columns. Set the first column ½" (1cm) wide; it is for the tab on which you'll place the tape. Set each of the remaining three columns 3⅝" (9cm) wide. In the three wide columns, the Gigi font was used at 72 pt for the word "table" and 90 pt for the table number. Print the wording on the green curlicue paper. Measure and mark the columns using the measurements above. With the ruler and the bone folder, score and fold the three fold lines.

3 Run a strip of double-sided tape down the tab, on the side of the paper with the printing. Stick the tab onto the back of the far right column, making a triangular prism.

TIP

When making projects that need to be assembled like this table card, use a double-sided tape that has a removable protective strip on one side. You can print and score each piece, place the tape on each tab ahead of time and transport the pieces flat. Then at the reception hall you just remove the strip from the tape and assemble the cards into their finished shape.

BLESSINGS & WISHES BOOKLET

This booklet is a fresh alternative to the traditional guest book, which typically includes only enough space for names and addresses. At your reception, place one booklet with a pen at each table, where guests can record not only their names but also warm wishes, congratulatory messages and words of wisdom.

what you will need

- 5" × 14" (13cm × 36cm) green cardstock
- 8½" × 11" (22cm × 28cm) lime green cardstock
- 11" × 17" (28cm × 43cm) off-white cardstock, 2 sheets
- felt leaf with beads (Marcel Schurman Do-Jiggies)
- 24" (61cm) of dark green embroidery floss
- green beads of various sizes and shapes

- scissors
- ruler
- pencil
- bone folder
- awl
- no. 18 blunt needle
- double-sided tape

1 Create a document for 2¾" × 3" (7cm × 8cm) label. Leave about 2" (5cm) between the two lines of wording. Here, the Gigi font was used at 18 pt. Print wording onto the lime green paper, and trim the label to size.

2 With a ruler and bone folder, fold the 5" × 14" (13cm × 36cm) cardstock in half to a size of 5" × 7" (13cm × 18cm).

3 Cut the off-white sheets to 5" × 14" (13cm × 36cm). Use the ruler and bone folder to fold each sheet in half to make 5" × 7" (13cm × 18cm) pages for the booklet.

4 Nest the sheets one inside the other. Take out the center page. On its fold, make pencil marks ½" (1cm) from the top of the page and ½" (1cm) from the bottom of the page. Make a third mark 2½" (6cm) from the top. Place the page back into the center of the other pages.

5 Nest the pages inside the cover. Make sure all folded edges are lined up properly and that the pieces are nested tightly together. Close the book just enough to form a V. Use the awl or needle to pierce through the pages and cover at the center of the V at each of the three marks. Make sure the tool is going through the fold of each piece.

6 Thread the embroidery floss into the eye of the needle so you have a 2" (5cm) to 3" (8cm) tail (just enough for you to hold the floss in the needle). To sew the book together, push the needle through the middle hole, going from the outside (cover side) of the book to the center, leaving a 5" (13cm) tail.

7 Push the needle through the bottom hole, going from the inside of the book to the outside. Pull the floss tight, but be sure that the tail remains 5" (13cm). (You may need to hold the tail in place for the first stitch or so.) Before making the next stitch, string a few beads onto the floss.

8 Push the needle through the top hole, going from the outside of the book to the inside. Pull the floss tight.

9 Push the needle through the middle hole, going from the inside of the book to the outside. Take care to not sew through the floss that is already in the hole. Pull the floss tight.

10 Place the two tails so that one is on each side of the long stitch. Arrange the beads on the long stitch the way you want them, then tie a knot with the two tails. Make sure all of the stitching is tight.

11 String beads onto the two tails, then knot the ends of each tail to secure the beads. Trim the floss to the desired length.

12 Cut a 2" (5cm) square from a scrap piece of dark green cardstock. Center it onto the printed lime green square and adhere it with double-sided tape. Remove the backing from the felt leaf sticker and place it in the center of the 2" (5cm) square. Center and adhere the finished label onto the cover of the booklet with double-sided tape.

ENCOURAGE CREATIVITY

Along with a blessings and wishes booklet at each table, include creative supplies that will enable your guests to really go wild. Colored pencils, crayons, decorative punches and various pieces of scrap paper are just some of the materials you could provide. Before the event, send a notice to guests asking them to bring a photo that depicts themselves with either the bride or the groom. Explain that they will be adding this photo and the thoughts it inspires to a booklet at the reception. To be more spontaneous and to preserve more memories of the event, have an attendant take instant pictures of the guests as they arrive, and have the guests add their messages next to those pictures.

MAKING A BEADED ACCENT

If you can't find the perfect beaded accent for your wedding papercrafts, try making your own. It can be as easy as cutting out a shape, applying an adhesive, and sprinkling on the beads. For the leaf accent shown in this project, cut out a leaf shape (pattern on page 123) from lime green handmade paper. Glue the leaf on dark green cardstock and cut ⅛" (3mm) away from the shape. With some gold dimensional paint, outline the leaf and add the center vein. Sprinkle the green bead mixture onto the wet paint. Let the paint dry completely.

BEADED POUCH FAVOR

As fun as it is functional, this eye-catching pouch is ideal for small or flat wedding favors. Use it to hold a lottery ticket, a leaf-shaped sugar cookie or even a small bag of bath salts or instant hot chocolate.

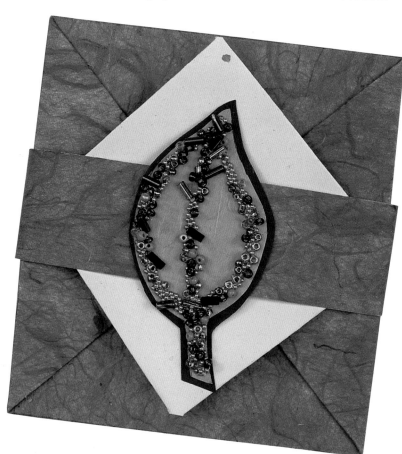

what you will **need**

- 8½" × 11" (22cm × 28cm) sage green handmade paper
- 8½" × 11" (22cm × 28cm) cream specked text-weight paper
- beaded leaf accent (see sidebar)
- craft knife
- cutting mat
- ruler
- bone folder
- spray adhesive
- glue stick
- pouch template (on page 122)

1 To make a contrasting lining for your pouch, fuse the sage green handmade paper and cream text-weight paper together with spray adhesive. With the ruler and craft knife, cut a 7" × 10½" (18cm × 27cm) paper piece and an 8" × 1" (20cm × 3cm) strip. Measure and score all the lines shown on the template for easy folding, and cut where indicated. Take your time and measure carefully and precisely.

2 Fold and crease along all scored lines. Reopen and flatten the paper piece. With what will be the inside of the pouch face down, fold each corner on the end flaps, forming an arrow shape. Glue these flaps down with the glue stick.

3 Pinch the corners together, then tuck them around to the sides with the pointed flaps, and glue them down under the pointed flap.

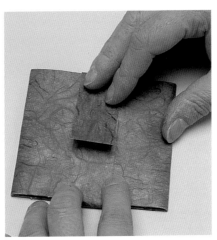

4 With your fingers, push in and "collapse" the top and bottom sides, pressing the pouch flat. Crease well.

5 Fashion the band by wrapping the paper strip around the pouch, then glue the overlap.

6 Glue the beaded leaf accent on the band. (Directions for making your own beaded leaf on opposite page.) Slip off the band and pull the pointed flaps outward to pop open the pouch and reveal its contents.

Because you have shared in our lives
by your friendship and love,
we

Leah Marie Holloway
and
Nathan Dale Streeter

together with our parents
Mr. & Mrs. Clarion Holloway
and
Mr. and Mrs. Donald Streeter
invite you to share
the beginning of our new life together
as we exchange marriage vows
Saturday, the first of May
Two thousand and two
at two o'clock in the afternoon

Grace Church
3254 Penn Avenue North
Minneapolis, Minnesota

Dessert reception
will follow in the
Fellowship Hall

fresh as a DAISY

Daisies evoke the wonderful carefree feeling of a spring day. When you choose daisies as a wedding theme, you welcome this cheerful feeling into your celebration. To round out the theme, incorporate fresh daisies into your floral arrangements.

These papercrafts set the stage for a morning or afternoon ceremony with a light, casual atmosphere. The varying hues of yellow and white are a perfect color combination for warm-weather festivities. With this sunny forecast, your guests can look forward to a spirited affair full of fun, friendship and happiness.

To the delight of all, daisies will be popping up everywhere throughout the celebration. The invitation includes a lovely pressed daisy, the photo album gift features a daisy pattern, and the table decorations consist of little vellum daisies. The flower girl basket and the paper bag vase are special projects that are sure to catch the eye of every guest!

INVITATION • FLOWER GIRL BASKET • PHOTO ALBUM GIFT • PAPER BAG GIFT • TABLE CONFETTI

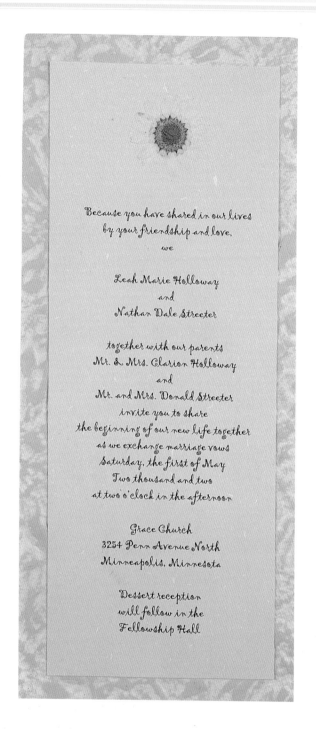

INVITATION

At the top of this invitation is a pressed daisy, extending a sweet and sentimental welcome to your guests. The embossed sheet of yellow paper echoes the daisy motif and sets a cheerful tone.

what you will need

- 8½" × 11" (22cm × 28cm) tan specked cardstock
- 22" × 30" (56cm × 76cm) embossed daisy paper
- no.10 envelope
- pressed white daisies (Real Flower Confetti-White Daisy)
- scissors
- ruler
- pencil
- paintbrush
- white craft glue

TIP

When layering with embossed paper, use glue instead of double-sided tape. The surface of embossed paper is so uneven that double-sided tape may not hold the paper securely.

---

1 Create a document for 3¾" × 8⅝" (10cm × 22cm) pieces. Center the wording horizontally, and begin 2" (5cm) from the top of the paper. Here the Gigi font was used at 12pt. Print the wording on the tan cardstock, and trim to size.

2 Place a small puddle of glue in a small bowl. Add one or two drops of water to the glue and mix with a damp brush. The glue mixture should be easy to brush onto the back of the pressed daisies. If the glue is too thick, it may pull the

petals out of the flower when you apply the glue to the back of the daisy. (Keep a wet cloth by your work area to clean any glue off your fingers. If they are sticky, the flower might stick to them, making it difficult to place the flower on the invitation.) Turn a daisy upside down, and gently paint the thinned glue on the center and the petals. Carefully glue it on the top of the invitation, centered between the top of the paper and the wording. Let the glue dry.

3 Cut the embossed daisy paper to 4" × 9¼" (10cm × 24cm).

4 Brush a thin coat of white glue over the surface of the back of the printed cardstock. Center the cardstock on the embossed paper. Gently smooth the surface of the paper, being careful not to damage the daisy. This invitation fits into a no. 10 envelope.

FLOWER GIRL BASKET

A flower girl pulling petals from this sweet conical basket will capture the hearts of all your wedding guests. Crafted from handmade petal paper, the basket can also be used to adorn church pews or hold flower blossoms at the reception.

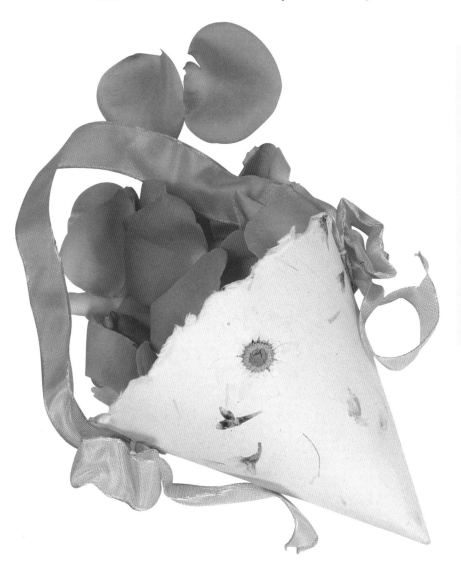

what you will need

- 8½" × 11" (22cm × 28cm) yellow cover-weight paper with pressed flowers
- 26" (66cm) of 1" (3cm) wide yellow grosgrain wired ribbon
- yellow or off-white thread
- pressed white daisies (Pressed Petals)
- scissors
- pencil
- paintbrush
- sewing needle
- white craft glue
- flower girl basket pattern (page 123)

1 Place the pattern onto the yellow paper so the straight edge of the pattern lines up with the edge of the paper.

2 Wet the paintbrush with water, and follow the curve of the template on the yellow paper with the brush. At this water line rip the yellow paper so the basket will have a deckle edge. Make sure the curve is sufficiently wet.

3 Bring the two ends of the paper together to make a cone. Overlap the paper, making sure the tip of the cone doesn't have a hole in it, and glue the edge with craft glue.

4 Press the ribbon if necessary. Thread a needle, double the thread, and tie a knot at the end. Starting at one end of the ribbon, go up 4" (10cm) and make a loop from the next 3" (8cm) of ribbon. Pinch the bottom of the loop between your fingers, and bring the long section of ribbon up toward the top of the loop so the 4" (10cm) tail hangs down and the long section of ribbon is going in the other direction. Holding the loop in place, push the threaded needle through the inside of the cone, about ½" (1cm) from the top edge. Guide

the thread around the pinched ribbon area and push the needle back into the cone. Repeat once to hold the ribbon securely. The tail of the ribbon should hang down, and the long length of ribbon should go up over the top of the basket. Leave a 12" (30cm) section of ribbon for the handle of the basket. Tie off the thread. Repeat the loop process, and sew it onto the cone basket at the opposite side.

5 Glue a pressed daisy to the front of the basket (see Invitation, step 2, on page 42).

PHOTO ALBUM GIFT

The cover of this album features an open square to frame a special photograph from the wedding day. Customize the covers to honor the recipients — they'll be thrilled to have pictures of themselves with the bride and groom!

what you will need

- 22" × 30" (56cm × 76cm) embossed daisy paper
- 11" × 17" (28cm × 43cm) off-white cardstock, 2 sheets
- 24" (61cm) of 1" (3cm) wide yellow grosgrain wired ribbon
- scissors
- metal ruler

- pencil
- bone folder
- craft knife
- cutting mat
- awl
- needle with eye the ribbon fits
- tape

1 Cut the embossed paper to 5" × 27" (13cm × 69cm). With a bone folder, fold the embossed paper in half so it measures 5" × 13½" (13cm × 34cm).

2 Open the folded piece. Score and measure 7" (18cm) to the left of the middle fold line. Fold the paper in toward the middle fold. Repeat this process on the right side of the middle fold. When you are finished you should have flaps on each side of the middle fold that are folded inward.

3 Open the flap on the left side of the middle fold line. Find the center of the 7" (18cm) panel with a ruler. Measure down 1" (3cm) from the top of the cover and make a mark 1" (3cm) to the right of the center of the panel and a mark 1" (3cm) to the left of the center of the panel. These two marks are top corners of the 2" (5cm) square opening in the cover. Next measure down 3" (8cm) from the top of the cover and make a mark 1" (3cm) to the right of the center of the panel and then mark 1" (3cm) to the left of the center of the panel. These two marks are the bottom corners of the square. Make your measurements accurately to get a true 2" (5cm) square opening. If it will help you cut the lines, you can lightly mark the lines in between the dots with a ruler and pencil. This will also help you check if your measuring is correct before you cut the square. You may want to practice cutting the square on a scrap of paper first.

4 Place the cover on the cutting mat. Place the ruler on the edge of the paper under the top two marks. Using the craft knife, carefully cut horizontally from one mark to the other.

5 Place the edge of the ruler on the left side of the two marks that are to the left of the center of the panel. Cut a vertical line between the marks using the craft knife.

6 Repeat steps 4 and 5 to cut the bottom horizontal line and the right vertical line, completing the square. Make sure your ruler is straight before making each cut, and cut all the way through the paper before moving the ruler. Set the cover aside.

7 Cut the off-white paper to 5" × 14" (13cm × 36cm) pieces. You should be able to get two from each sheet. With a bone folder, score and fold the four sheets in half to make the pages 5" × 7" (13cm × 8cm).

8 Nest the sheets inside each other. Take out the center page. On the fold, make a pencil mark ½" (1cm) from the top of the pages and ½" (1cm) up from the bottom of the page. Make a third mark 2½" (6cm) from the top. Place the page back into the center of the other pages.

9 Nest the pages inside the cover. Make sure all folded edges are lined up properly and that they are nested tightly together. Close the book just enough to form a V. Pierce through the pages with the awl and cover at the center of the V at each of the three marked places. Make sure the awl goes through the folds of all the sheets of paper.

10 Thread the ribbon into the needle, and leave a tail a few inches long. To sew the book together, start on the outside of the book. Push the needle through the middle hole, going from the outside of the book to the inside, and leave an 8" (20cm) tail.

11 Push the needle through the bottom hole, from the inside of the book to the outside. Pull the ribbon tight; make sure there is no twist in the ribbon and that it is flat. You may need to hold the tail in place for the first stitch or more to keep the tail 8" (20cm) long.

12 Make a long stitch to the top hole on the outside of the book. Push the needle through the hole, going from the outside of the book through to the inside. Pull the ribbon tight, again making sure there is no twist in the ribbon.

13 Push the needle through the middle hole, from the inside of the book to the outside. Make sure you do not sew through the ribbon that is already through the hole. Pull the ribbon tight, with no twists.

14 Take the needle off of the ribbon. Place one ribbon tail on each side of the long stitch and tie a bow. Trim the ends of the ribbon. Insert a photo under the flap of the front cover, and position it so it shows through the cut window. Tape it on the back to secure.

PHOTO CHECKLIST

To be sure your wedding is captured as completely as you want it to be, make a check list of the shots that are most important to you and give it to your photographer or to a friend who is assisting with snapshots. Following are some suggestions for the checklist:

- Getting ready for the ceremony, putting on the veil, and the garter
- Each member of the wedding party coming down the aisle
- The bride and father preparing for their walk down the aisle
- The ring exchange
- The kiss
- The new couple's walk from the altar
- Arrival of bride and groom to the reception
- Toasting the couple
- The first dance
- The cutting of the cake
- Tossing the bouquet
- Removing/tossing the garter
- Leaving for the honeymoon

PAPER BAG VASE

This unique centerpiece, a plain paper bag converted into a watertight vase, is sure to be met with many "ooohs" and "ahhhs"! Your guests won't believe that this paper bag, stamped and embossed with the daisy motif, actually holds water and flowers!

what you will ***need***

- white paper bag
- white pigment stamp pad
- daisy rubber stamp (Rubber Stampede)
- clear embossing powder
- sheer yellow ribbon
- white button
- decorative-edge scissors
- latex gloves
- spray can
- mixing cups and mixing sticks
- disposable paintbrushes
- rubber band
- heat gun
- waxed paper
- masking tape
- pour-on two-part polymer coating, 6 ounces (172g) per bag (EnviroTex Lite)
- craft glue

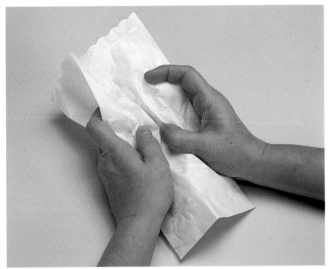

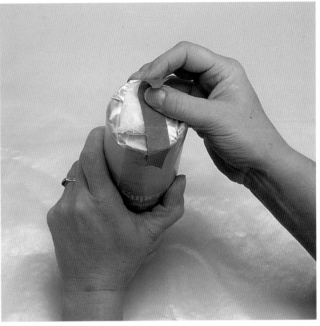

1 Stamp the daisy motif on the bag with the white pigment ink pad. Do only three daisies at a time to make sure the ink does not dry before embossing. Sprinkle on clear embossing powder. Tap off the excess powder onto a sheet of paper. Heat the embossing powder until melted with the heat gun (see Thermal Embossing, page 119). Crumble up the bag slightly to give it interesting folds and wrinkles. Use decorative-edge scissors to trim the top of the bag.

2 Cover a spray can with waxed paper. Use masking tape to hold the waxed paper around the can.

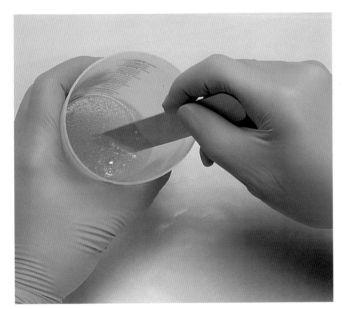

3 This process tends to be a bit messy. Wear protective gloves for the first pouring. Also cover your work area well with waxed paper. Follow the manufacturer's directions and mix 3 ounces (86g) of polymer coating. Mix well for a full two minutes to make sure the hardener and resin are well mixed. Do not worry about any bubbles — they are supposed to form.

4 Place the bag over the covered spray can, making sure the bottom is straight. Pour the mixed polymer onto the bag. Brush it down the sides of the bag. The bag will look wet, making it easy to spot missed areas.

5 Once the bag is completely covered, place a rubber band around the bag to shape the vase. Adjust the bag to get the shape you want. The rubber band usually peels off, but use a light-colored one in case it sticks to the resin.

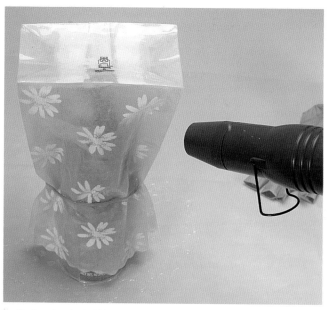

6 Pop the the bubbles with the heat gun (the heat will pop them), and put the coated bag in a dust-free area to set for twelve hours. Discard the gloves, foam brush, mixing container and stir stick.

7 After the bag has cured, remove it from the base by giving the bag a gentle twist to release it. Set it on the waxed paper. The bag will be very flexible. Make sure the base is sitting flat on the table, and adjust the form of the bag if you wish. Mix a second mixture of 3 ounces (86g) of polymer coating and pour it into the bag.

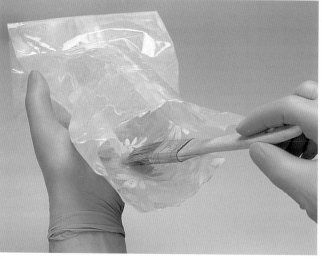

8 Brush the polymer coating up the sides of the bag to completely cover the inside. This second coating makes the bag strong with thick walls. The excess will also pool in the bottom of the bag to create a sturdy base. Pop the bubbles with the heat gun. Set in a dust-free area to set for another twelve hours. Discard the brush, mixing container and mixing stick. Tie a tailored bow from the ribbon and trim the ends (see Tailored Bow, page 121). Glue a white button to the center of the bow and glue the bow onto the vase.

TABLE CONFETTI

What better way to spread the warmth of the daisy theme than with confetti? Sprinkled on the reception tables, these bright daisies add a bit of joy to the celebration.

STAMPING BASICS

Using rubber stamps is a quick and easy way to add your own unique touch to your wedding papercrafts. Here are a few tips that will help you make a great impression with stamps:

- When working with a large stamp, ink the stamp by tapping the pad several times on the stamp. Pressing the stamp hard into the pad can overink the stamp and make a messy image.

- Press the stamp onto the paper on a firm, smooth surface. Do not rock the stamp, just use firm downward pressure to ensure a clean, crisp image.

- To clean the stamp, dab stamp cleaner onto the stamp, then stamp on a layer of several paper towels to remove the ink. Make sure the stamp is dry before inking it and making another image.

what you will need

- 8½" × 11" (22cm × 28cm) cream vellum paper for approximately 24 daisies, 1½" (4cm) diameter each
- white pigment stamp pad
- daisy rubber stamp (template to hand carve on page 123)
- clear embossing powder
- yellow marker
- scissors
- heat gun

1 Stamp the daisy motif on the cream vellum sheets with the white pigment ink pad. Do only three daisies at a time so the ink does not dry before the next step.

2 Color the flower centers in with the yellow marker. Immediately sprinkle on clear embossing powder. Tap off the excess powder onto a sheet of paper.

3 Heat the embossing powder until melted with the heat gun.

4 Cut the daisies out with the scissors, leaving a ⅛" (3cm) border around each flower.

Josie and Sean

joining together

as one

in Christ

Please kindly reply by
...ber 20, 2002

...nding

Josie Cartellone
and
Sean Kinnear

October 5, 2002
Hollywood Roosevelt Hotel
Hollywood, California

steeped in
CELTIC CHARM

Many brides and grooms choose to celebrate their heritage as part of their wedding ceremony. In this set, the Irish ancestry of the groom was the inspiration for an elegant Celtic theme. With its medieval and mythical associations, a Celtic theme captures the enchantment of ancient romance. Soft greens and ochres, a distinctive font, and Celtic designs generate an antique feeling that is well suited for either a large formal affair or a quaint, intimate gathering.

Renowned for its complex knot work, Celtic art offers an endless supply of motifs. Use stamps with these motifs to unify all the elements of the set, and keep the stamps to later design your thank-you cards or personal stationery. Your handcrafted invitation, wedding program, and pinwheel favor will not just welcome your guests to your special day, but also transport them into a magical Celtic world.

INVITATION · PROGRAM · BLESSINGS & WISHES BOOKLET · PINWHEEL FAVOR · LUMINARY

INVITATION

An important design element in this simple trifold invitation is the Celtic knot, with its intricate interweaving of a single unbroken line. The knot, which represents the continuity of the universe and the interconnectedness of all life, is a perfect symbol for the joining of two lives in marriage.

Josie and Sean

joining together

as one

in Christ

Don't walk in front of me,
I may not follow.

Don't walk behind me,
I may not lead.

Walk beside me,
and be my friend.

-Irish Proverb

Josie Cartellone
and
Sean Kinnear
invite you to the joyous
celebration of the joining
together of their hearts
in marriage
on Saturday, October 5th, 2002
at six in the evening
at Hollywood Roosevelt Hotel
at 7000 Hollywood Boulevard
Hollywood, California

Dinner and dancing will

Please kindly reply by
September 20, 2002

Number attending _____

Name _____

- 8½" × 11" (22cm × 28cm) off-white flecked cardstock, 2 sheets
- no. 10 envelope
- no. 4 envelope
- light green metallic inkpad
- Celtic square rubber stamp (All Night Media)
- Celtic circle sealing stamp (JudiKins)
- small Celtic cross rubber stamp (All Night Media)
- large Celtic cross rubber stamp (JudiKins)
- gold cross charm on "O" ring
- brass clipiola paper clip
- scissors
- ruler
- bone folder
- heat gun (optional)

SENDING INVITATIONS

Postage is important to consider when you are figuring out the size and the cost of your invitations. Most envelopes meet the requirements for the standard letter rate. Note the following instances that may cost you more than the standard rate:

- The envelope is smaller than 3½" × 5" (9cm × 13cm) or is bigger than 6⅛" × 11½" (16cm × 29cm).
- The envelope is square.
- The envelope has a clasp, string, buttons or similar closure device.
- The envelope weighs 1 ounce (29g) or more.
- The envelope is too bulky to run through the postal machine any requires hand cancellation.
- Anything that might cause the surface of the letter to be uneven might cost you extra postage.

1 Create a document in a landscape orientation with three equal columns. On one side, put the proverb in the left column, leave the center column blank, and use the right column as the invitation cover. Put the main wording in the center column of the other side. The font used here was Stonehenge. Start the proverb (13pt) 2⅝" (7cm) from the top. The cover wording (16pt) starts 5½" (14cm) from the top, and the main wording (14pt) on side two starts 2⅜" (6cm) from the top. The text color used here was dark green. Print the invitation on the off-white cardstock.

2 With the main wording face up, measure 3⅝" (9cm) from the left edge and make pencil marks at the top and bottom. Score this line with a bone folder. Fold the left side toward the center of the paper. From the fold line measure over another 3⅝" (9cm) and score and fold again in toward the center. The right flap goes under the left flap.

3 Ink and stamp the large Celtic cross on the cover. Center the cross between the top of the card and the lettering. Allow the ink to dry (a heat gun speeds the process).

4 Ink the small Celtic cross and stamp it on the center section above the main wording. Center it between the top of the card and the wording. Allow the ink to dry.

5 Create a document for a 3½ " × 5" (9cm × 13cm) card. Center the text on the card, using the same font at 13pt. Print the response card on the second sheet of cardstock, and trim to size. Ink and stamp the Celtic square stamp between the top of the card and the lettering. Allow the ink to dry.

6 Put the cross charm on the clipiola. Put the response card under the flap of the return envelope (a no. 4 envelope). Clip the response card and envelope inside the top of the right flap. A no. 10 envelope fits this invitation.

If you have any questions or doubts about what the cost for mailing your invitation will be, take a sample with all the different enclosures in the envelope to the post office. They will be able to determine what the postage will be for each invitation.

Postcards (for your response cards or thank you's) can be no smaller than 3½" × 5" (9cm × 13cm) and no bigger than 4¼" × 6" (11cm × 15cm). Postcards need to be printed on 65–80lb (140gsm to 170gsm) paper. For more information, check out the United States Postal Service Web site at www.usps.com.

WIRE CLIPS

It is easy to form wire into your own decorative wire fasteners for clipping papers together or closing packages. Use 18-gauge colored copper wire that is found in craft stores. Coil and form the wire pieces with needle-nose pliers. Use a wire cutter to trim the wire.

Alternatively, you can coil wire with a clear peg-type jig. Simply place the clear jig over the desired design, align the pegs with the turns in the design, and form the pieces with the wire. This method is very useful when making more than one piece. After forming the wire, flatten the piece with a hammer on a hard, flat surface. The flattened pieces will be stronger and hold the paper better.

PROGRAM

In addition to providing ceremony information, this program features a tear-off bookmark that guests can keep as a memento. Choose a Celtic verse or saying that is meaningful to you, or replace the text with a beautiful Celtic design.

Josie Cartellone
and
Sean Kinnear

October 5, 2002
Hollywood Roosevelt Hotel
Hollywood, California

what you will need

- 8½" × 11" (22cm × 28cm) off-white flecked cardstock
- 8½" × 11" (22cm × 28cm) moss green text-weight paper
- light green metallic ink pad
- large Celtic cross rubber stamp (JudiKins)
- two ⅛" (3mm) olive green eyelets
- scissors
- ruler
- pencil
- bone folder
- ⅛" (3mm) hole punch
- eyelet setter
- hammer
- rotary cutter with perforating blade
- cutting mat
- double-sided tape

TIP

If you'd like to perforate paper but don't have a perforating tool, use your sewing machine instead. Without any thread in the machine, "sew" along the line you'd like to perforate. The holes formed by the needle will make the paper easy to tear.

The Wedding Ceremony of
Josie Cartellone and Sean Kinnear

Prelude...Water Music

Processional.........Jesus, Joy of Man's Desiring
                        Trumpet Voluntary

Invocation

Brief Words to Bride and Groom

Solo...I Will be There

Intention of Marriage

Exchange of Vows and Rings

Communion

Solo...The Lord's Prayer

Benediction

Presentation of Mr. and Mrs. Kinnear

The W

Officiating Priest

Maid of Honor....

Bridesmaids.............
Terry Wessleman

Best Man.............

Groomsmen.............
Ryan Kinnear, M

Flower Girl.............

Ring Bearer.............

Pianist.............

Soloist.............

May the
road rise to
meet you.
May the wind
always be at
your back.
May the sun
shine warm
upon your
face;
the rains fall
soft upon your
fields
and until we
meet again,
may God hold
you in the
palm of
His hand.

1 Cut the off-white cardstock to 7" × 11" (18cm × 22cm). Create a two-page landscape document, printed on two sides. Format the first side with three columns set at, from left to right, 4¼" (11cm), 4¼" (11cm) and 2½" (6cm). Print the program information in the two wide columns on one side of the cardstock. Format the second side with two columns, the left set at 6½" (17cm) and the right at 4½" (11cm). Print the front cover information in the right-hand column on the other side. (The bookmark information is printed in step 4.) The font Stonehenge was used here in sizes 14pt and 16pt.

2 With the inside of the program facing up, measure 4¼" (11cm) from the left side and mark. Score and fold the cardstock with the ruler and the bone folder.

3 With the inside of the program facing up, place the program on a cutting mat. Measure 2⁵⁄₁₆" (6cm) from the right edge. Align the ruler at that distance and run the rotary cutter with the perforating blade along this line to perforate the bookmark.

4 Create a 2" × 6½" (5cm × 17cm) document. Center the wording 1⅛" (3cm) from the top, using the same font at 16pt. Print the Irish blessing onto the moss green paper.

5 With the program open flat and the cover facing up, adhere the bookmark inlay to the center of the bookmark section with double-sided tape. Make a mark ⅝" (2cm) down from the top of the bookmark in the center, and punch a hole. Place one eyelet in the hole and set (see Setting Eyelets, page 118). Measure ⅝" (2cm) from the bottom and set one eyelet there. Ink and stamp the large Celtic cross on to the cover of the program, centering the cross between the top of the program and the wording. Let dry.

BLESSINGS & WISHES BOOKLET

*Friends and family will enjoy the opportunity to write personal messages to the bride
and groom in this handcrafted booklet. As the married couple celebrates their anniversary
every year they can look at the books together and share memories of the occasion.*

BLESSINGS AND WISHES
FOR
JOSIE AND SEAN

what you will need

- 11" × 17" (28cm × 43cm) moss green cardstock
- 11" × 17" (28cm × 43cm) off-white flecked cardstock, 2 sheets
- 8½" × 11" (22cm × 28cm) off-white cardstock
- 8½" × 11" (22cm × 28cm) medium green cardstock
- 8½" × 11" (22cm × 28cm) gold metallic text-weight paper
- 24" (61cm) of ½" (1cm) green ribbon
- cross charm with "O" ring

- needle with eye the ribbon fits
- bookbinding awl
- scissors
- ruler
- pencil
- bone folder
- double-sided tape
- white craft glue

TIP

A quick and easy way to trim and
punch many pieces of paper is to take
them to your local copy shop. Provide
them with an exact template of how
you would like the paper cut and where
to place the holes.

1 Create a document with an area that's 1⅝" × 3⅝" (4cm × 9cm). Start the wording ½" (1cm) from the top and center the text. The Stonehenge font was used here at 16pt. Print the front panel onto off-white cardstock.

2 Cut the medium green cardstock to 2" × 4" (5cm × 10cm) and the gold cardstock to 1¾" × 3¾" (4.5cm × 9.5cm). Layer the printed paper onto the gold paper and the gold paper onto the green paper using double-sided tape, centering each. Set aside.

3 Cut the two sheets of flecked cardstock to 5" × 14" (13cm × 36cm) pieces, yielding two per sheet. With a bone folder and ruler, score and fold the four sheets in half to make the pages 5" × 7" (13cm × 18cm). Nest the sheets one inside the other.

4 Take the center page out. On the fold, make pencil marks ½" (1cm) from the top and ½" (1cm) from the bottom. Make a third mark 2½" (6cm) from the top. Place the page back into the center of the pages.

5 Cut the moss green cardstock to 5" × 14½" (13cm × 37cm). With a bone folder and ruler, score and fold the cardstock in half to make the cover 5" × 7¼" (13cm × 18cm).

6 Tightly nest the pages inside the cover, making sure the edges align. Close the book just enough to form a V. Use the awl or a needle to pierce through the pages and cover on the fold at each of the three marked places.

7 Thread the needle with the ribbon, leaving a tail of a few inches. Sew the book together, starting on the outside of the book and pushing the needle through the middle hole. Leave an 8" (20cm) tail of ribbon.

8 Push the needle through the bottom hole from the inside of the book to the outside. Pull the ribbon tight, making sure the ribbon is flat. Hold the tail so that it does not become shorter than 8" (20cm).

9 Push the needle through the top hole from the outside of the book to the inside. Pull the ribbon tight, again making sure there is no twist in the ribbon.

10 Push the needle through the middle hole, from the inside of the book to the outside. Do not sew through the ribbon that is already there. Pull the ribbon tight with no twists.

11 Remove the needle from the ribbon and set it aside. Place one tail of the ribbon on each side of the long stitch.

12 Place the charm on an "O" ring. Tie a half knot, then slip the "O" ring with the charm onto one of the ribbon ends. Slide the charm up to the half-knot, then finish tying a shoestring bow (see Shoestring Bow, page 120). Trim the ends of the ribbon. For extra security, put a small dab of craft glue on the half-knot after you slip on the charm.

13 Center the label onto the cover of the booklet and adhere it with double-sided tape.

ADDING PHOTOS
TO YOUR GUEST BOOK

Place one or two single-use cameras on each of the guest tables at your reception. Your guests will have a great time capturing candid and intimate moments that a busy professional photographer might miss. Have guests drop the exposed cameras into a basket near the exit as they leave. Before the honeymoon, you can drop off the cameras to be developed and when you come back you can see what a nice time your guests had at your wedding. The photos can then be added to your guest book, with the guests' photos near their sentiments. It might be a good idea to add several pages to the book and mark them ahead of time as "reserved for photos."

PINWHEEL FAVOR

When unfolded, this package takes on the shape of a pinwheel resembling Saint Brigid's cross, a symbol traditionally hung over the doorway of Irish homes to ward off want and evil. According to one legend, Saint Brigid was the patroness of chivalrous knights, who invoked her name when they began calling the women they were to marry "brides."

what you will need

- 12" (30cm) square off-white cardstock
- 12" (30cm) square decorative green text-weight paper
- 8½" × 11" (22cm × 28cm) off-white cardstock
- 2" (5cm) square glassine envelope (to hold seeds of your choice)
- tassel and string, about 4" (10cm) long
- stamped polymer clay seal (see page 116)
- scissors
- ruler
- pencil
- bone folder
- glue stick
- glue gun with clear glue stick
- pinwheel pattern (on page 122)

1 Cut two 4" × 12" (10cm × 30cm) pieces from the 12" (30cm) off-white cardstock. Cut the decorative paper to 3¾" × 11¾" (9.5cm × 29.5cm). Adhere the decorative paper to one of the off-white pieces with a glue stick.

2 Use the pattern to cut and score this piece. Cut and score the second off-white piece of cardstock in the same way.

3 Place the decorative piece face down, then place the second off-white piece on top of it to form a pinwheel. Glue the center square pieces together using a glue stick.

4 Cut one 1¼" × 10" (3cm × 25m) strip from both the off-white cardstock and the decorative paper. Glue these together and set aside.

5 Print the thank-you message on the 8½" × 11" (22cm × 28cm) off-white cardstock. Create a document for a card that measures 3" × 2½" (8cm × 6cm). Center the text ¼" (6mm) from the top. The font Stonehenge was used here at 12pt. A fine-line border was also added.

6 Glue the thank-you panel to the center of the center square and place the little envelope of seeds on top.

7 Fold the points over, slipping the fourth point under the first point to form the package.

8 Wrap the strip around the package, and using a glue stick, glue the ends together where they overlap in the back.

9 With the glue gun, center the tassel and the seal to the paper strip in the front of the package (see Making Tassels, page 117, and Making Polymer Clay Seals, page 116).

LUMINARY

When illuminated, this paper-covered glass cylinder generates a romantic atmosphere by casting a warm glow over the reception tables. You can vary the effect by using the glass vessel to hold flowers or a floating candle instead of a pillar candle.

TIP

Seals add an elegant and unique touch to any wedding papercrafts. While polymer clay seals will hold up to just about anything, traditional wax seals are more fragile. If you mail a piece with a wax seal, write "Hand Cancel" on the outside because the seal will be brittle and may not survive the postal sorting machine.

1 Cut the green paper to 12" × 18" (30cm × 46cm), then tear this sheet into pieces approximately 4" (10cm) square. Cut a 2" × 15" (5cm × 38cm) strip from the cream paper with the deckle-edged scissors. Set aside.

2 Clean the glass with rubbing alcohol and a clean cloth; let dry. Start with the torn pieces of paper that have a straight edge. Découpage them around the top edge of the glass cylinder using the découpage medium and flat brush. Overlap the pieces for complete coverage. Cover the entire cylinder, including the bottom, with the green paper.

3 Découpage the cream strip of paper around the cylinder, 1½" (4cm) from the top. Let dry.

4 Cut a group of fibers to just fit around the vase. Place the fibers around the center of the cream band, tie a knot and glue the knot with hot glue. Use hot glue to attach the tassel to the front of the vase. Glue the tassel suspension cord to the back of a polymer clay stamped seal (see Making Polymer Clay Seals, page 116). Finish by gluing the polymer clay seal and tassel to the vase.

Cheryl Ann Manning
and
Bruce Alan Lyke
request the honor
of your presence
at their marriage
on Saturday,
the twenty-fifth of October
Two thousand and three
at two in the afternoon
Jesus People Church
2400 Nicollet Avenue South
Minneapolis, Minnesota

Please join us
for the
reception following
the ceremony in
Fellowship Hall

Music from
Cheryl and Bruce's
Wedding

October 25, 2003

the favor of a reply is requested
before October 11, 2003

regrets

a statement of COLOR

Sometimes beautiful color is all you need to make a lasting impression. For a classic wedding theme that is incredibly versatile, simply focus on color. The beauty of these projects lies in the dramatic contrast of rich burgundy and soft ivory, a lovely color combination for a fall or winter wedding. Feel free, however, to make modifications. If your wedding is to be held in the spring or summer months, consider using brighter colors for an equally eye-catching contrast. You can choose hues that either echo or complement the colors in your bouquet, attendants' dresses and other ceremony details.

Your guests will admire the burgundy corrugated paper, which blends richness of color with richness of texture. Created as keepsakes for the wedding guests, the gift candle, CD holder and pocket bookmark are all special treasures crafted from this paper. Your own treasure will be the guest book, a memento of your wedding day signed by well-wishing friends and family.

INVITATION • GUEST BOOK • CD KEEPSAKE • GIFT CANDLE • POCKET BOOKMARK

INVITATION

The custom-made pocket of this invitation can accommodate many additional components.
For a variation, print the text on heavier handmade paper with leaves or petals embedded in the pulp.

Cheryl Ann Manning
and
Bruce Alan Lyke
request the honor
of your presence
at their marriage
on Saturday,
the twenty-fifth of October
Two thousand and three
at two in the afternoon
Jesus People Church
2400 Nicollet Avenue South
Minneapolis, Minnesota

Please join us
for the
reception following
the ceremony in
Fellowship Hall

The favor of a reply is requested
before October 11, 2003

Name_____ regrets
_____ accepts _____

what you will need

- 26" × 40" (66cm × 102cm) burgundy corrugated paper
- 12" (30cm) square salmon leaf translucent paper
- 12" (30cm) square salmon leaf text-weight paper
- 8½" × 11" (22cm × 28cm) burgundy cardstock
- 6" × 9" (15cm × 23cm) envelope
- no. 4 envelope
- four ⅛" (3mm) antique brass eyelets
- 19" (48cm) of burgundy raffia
- scissors
- ruler
- pencil
- bone folder
- ⅛" (3mm) hole punch
- eyelet setter
- hammer
- cutting mat
- double-sided tape

1 Create a document 4½" × 7" (11cm × 18cm). Start the words ½" (1cm) from the top. The font Papyrus was used here, with the names of the bride and groom at 18pt and the rest at 14pt. Print the invitation on the salmon leaf paper, and trim to 4½" × 7" (11cm × 18cm).

2 Create a document 3" × 4½" (8cm × 11cm). Start the wording 1" (3cm) from the top, using the same font at 16pt. Print the response card on the salmon leaf text paper, and trim to size.

3 Cut the burgundy cardstock to 3½" × 5" (9cm × 13cm). With double-sided tape, stick the printed response card to the center of the burgundy cardstock.

4 Cut a 5" × 18½" (13cm × 47cm) piece of burgundy corrugated paper so that the corrugation lines run parallel to the long length of the paper.

5 Place the cut piece of the corrugated paper horizontally on a cutting mat with the smooth side up. Measure 2½" (6cm) from the right end of the corrugated paper, and mark the top and bottom of the paper. Score and fold the paper with a bone folder. This flap is the pocket of the invitation.

6 With the flap folded up, punch a hole ¼" (6mm) from the left edge and ¼" (6mm) from the top of the pocket. Repeat on the right hand side of the pocket. Place the eyelets in the holes and set them (see Setting Eyelets, page 118) to create the pocket.

7 With the corrugated paper still horizontal on the cutting surface, measure 8" (20cm) from the left edge of the paper to form the cover flap on the invitation. Mark the bottom and the top of the paper then score and fold at the 8" (20cm) marks.

8 Put double-sided tape on the back of the printed invitation paper and stick it onto the inside center of the 8" (20cm) panel on the smooth side of the corrugated paper. Place the enclosures in the pocket with the response card on top.

9 Cut a 2" × 9" (5cm × 23cm) band from the translucent paper. With the right side of the translucent paper up, punch one hole ½" (1cm) in from each end of the band and centered in the width of the band. Place an eyelet in each hole and set them.

10 Measure in 2" (5cm) on each end of the band and gently fold the ends in toward each other (do not make a hard crease). Slip this around the finished corrugated invitation, with the open side at the front of the invitation. Put one end of the raffia down into the left eyelet and pull it up through the right eyelet. Gently pull both ends of the raffia until the ends are the same length and the band is taut around the invitation. Tie the raffia into a bow. Trim the ends if necessary. This invitation fits in a 6" × 9" (15cm × 23cm) envelope; the response card fits into a no. 4 envelope.

TIP

Instead of using the 12" (30cm) square salmon leaf papers, listed for each of the projects in this chapter, consider carving your own leaf motif stamp and making your own printed paper. (See Carving Stamps, page 118, and use the leaf pattern on page 123.)

GUEST BOOK

Nothing reflects your attention to detail better than a beautifully crafted guest book. As your guests sign the book, they will no doubt admire your hard work and creativity — and never even guess how easy the book is to make!

what you will need

- 8½" × 11" (22cm × 28cm) burgundy cardstock, 3 sheets
- 8½" × 11" (22cm × 28cm) cream cardstock, 2 sheets
- 8½" × 11" (22cm × 28cm) cream text-weight paper, 10-12 sheets
- soft rose pigment ink pad

- leaf stamp
- 36" (91cm) of ¼" (6mm) wide burgundy wired ribbon
- decorative burgundy fibers
- gold heart charms
- scissors

- ruler
- pencil
- bone folder
- ¼" (6mm) hole punch
- large needle
- clamps

- scrap pieces of mat board
- paintbrush
- paper crimper
- glue stick
- white craft glue

1 Cut one piece of cream cardstock in half to get two 5½" × 8½" (14cm × 22cm) sheets. Using a ready-made stamp or a stamp you have carved yourself, stamp the end paper pieces using a soft rose ink pad. Stamp the motifs all over in a random pattern. Be sure to stamp some of the images off the edge of the paper.

2 Cut the text-weight sheets in half to get twenty to thirty 5½" × 8½" (14cm × 22cm) pages. Punch three holes in the end of each page. To do this by hand, make a template with one page. Punch the outer holes at least 1" (3cm) from each edge and center the third hole between the first two.

3 Wrap the pages of the book tightly with a scrap piece of paper to hold them even and secure, leaving the holes exposed. Brush a thin layer of white craft glue across the paper ends. Let dry completely. This creates a pad of pages that won't move out of place as you cover them.

4 Cut two pieces of burgundy cardstock to 6" × 9" (15cm × 23cm) for the covers. With a glue stick, glue the stamped end paper pieces to the back of the burgundy covers. Burnish well with the bone folder to make a strong bond.

5 Using a punched page as a template, punch holes in the cover pieces.

6 Score a fold line on the inside of the front cover, about 1" (3cm) from the left side, using the bone folder and a ruler. This scored line will enable guests to open the book smoothly.

7 Place the pages between the covers, making sure all the holes line up. Place scrap pieces of mat board on the back and front cover to prevent the covers from being marred, and use clamps to hold the book together.

8 Thread a large needle with the ribbon. Leaving a 5" (13cm) tail, push the needle and ribbon up through the top hole, going from the back of the book to the front. Push the needle down through the center hole, bring the ribbon around the outside edge of the book, and push the needle back down through the same hole. (Push the ribbon aside as you repeatedly go through the holes so that you don't pierce it. Be careful not to twist the ribbon as you bind the book.) Pull the needle up through the bottom hole, bring the ribbon around the outside edge of the book and push the needle up through the same hole. Wrap the ribbon down around the bottom edge and come up through the bottom hole once more. Push the needle down through the center hole then back up through the top hole. Bring the ribbon around the outside edge of the book and come back up through the top hole. Pull the ribbon toward the top edge of the book and tie it in a knot with the tail left in the back. Trim the ends close to the knot and dot the knot with craft glue.

9 Trim a piece of burgundy cardstock to 1¼" × 5½" (3cm × 14cm), then crimp this strip with the paper crimper.

10 Create a document for a 2" × 4½" (5cm × 11cm) label. Center the text. Again the font Papyrus was used here. Print the wording on cream cardstock, and trim the label to size.

11 Cut a piece of cream cardstock to 2½" × 5" (6cm × 13cm) and stamp it randomly with the soft rose ink and the leaf stamp. Cut a piece of burgundy cardstock to 2¼" × 4¾" (6cm × 12cm).

12 To decorate the front of the book, use craft glue to adhere the crimped paper strip to the left side of the book. Layer and glue the stamped panel, burgundy panel and panel with the lettering in place with a glue stick. Cut a small handful of the decorative fibers about 18" (46cm) long. Thread the fibers through the binding at the top of the book and knot them.

13 Accent the fibers by tying gold heart charms to the ends.

USING A PAPER CRIMPER

Using a paper crimper is a great way to add texture to paper. Insert the edge of the paper between the metal barrels, then squeeze the handles to grip the paper. Turn the key to move the paper through the barrels to crimp. To prevent drifting, mark a guide on the edge with a piece of masking tape. As the paper goes through, make sure it is lined up square to the guide edge for perfect crimps. If the paper edge starts to drift, release the handles slightly and realign the paper.

TIP

When tying a knot with fibers, it's helpful to wrap them around a crochet hook. The crochet hook keeps the fibers gathered so that all of them go through the loop of the knot together.

CD KEEPSAKE

After spending so much time compiling the perfect compact disc for your wedding day, create a holder that is worthy of its contents. With this simply designed CD holder, your "memory music" will be protected for years to come!

Music from
Cheryl and Bruce's
Wedding

October 25, 2003

what you will need

- 26" × 40" (66cm × 102cm) burgundy corrugated paper
- 12" (30cm) square salmon leaf text-weight paper
- 8½" × 11" (22cm × 28cm) off-white cardstock
- 8½" × 11" (22cm × 28cm) burgundy cardstock
- 8½" burgundy raffia
- six ⅛" (3mm) antique brass eyelets
- ⅛" (3mm) long-reach hole punch
- 1" (3cm) circle punch
- ½" (1cm) circle punch
- eyelet setter
- hammer
- cutting mat
- scissors
- ruler
- pencil
- bone folder
- double-sided tape
- CD template (page 123)

1 Create a document for a 3½" (9cm) square label. Start the words 1" (3cm) down from the top of the label. The font used here was Papyrus at 18pt for the names and 16pt for the remaining text. Print the CD holder label on the salmon leaf paper, and trim to size.

2 Cut the corrugated paper using the CD holder template. Score and fold the lines as shown on the template with the bone folder. Center the label on the front of the CD holder, and use double-sided tape to adhere it.

3 Place the CD holder open and completely flat with the corrugated side up on the cutting mat. Punch a hole about ⅛" (3mm) from the sides of one corner of the label. Place an eyelet in the hole and set it (see Setting Eyelets, page 118). Repeat the process in the other three corners.

4 Punch two circles out of the burgundy cardstock with the 1" (3cm) circle punch. Punch two circles out of the off-white cardstock with the ½" (1cm) circle punch. Place a small circle on top of a large circle and punch an ⅛" (3mm) hole in the center of the two circles. Repeat with the other set of circles.

5 Place the CD holder back down on the mat, open and flat. Measure ¾" (2cm) from the top of the flap and make a mark centered between the two outer edges. Punch one hole at this mark. Place one end of the raffia ½" (1cm) through the punched hole. Place one set of circles over the hole and put one eyelet through the circles and the paper. Set the eyelet. Make sure the raffia stays in the hole when you set the eyelet. This will attach the string to the flap.

6 Measure 2¼" (6cm) down from the top of the back panel, and center the mark between the outer edges. Punch one hole at the mark. Place the other set of circles over the hole and put the eyelet through the circles and the paper. Set the eyelet.

7 Before you assemble the CD holder, feel the back of the eyelets. If they feel rough, cover them with tape or something smooth so they won't scratch the CD. Fold the two side tabs of the holder in and place glue or double-sided tape on the tabs. Fold up the back of the holder onto the two tabs. If you used glue, place a heavy object (e.g., a large book) on top of the holder as it dries. You can use hook and loop fastener stickers on the flap and the back of the CD holder to hold the flap down instead of the string and layered circles.

SELECTING EYELETS AND BRADS

The selection of eyelets and brads that are now available is staggering. Not only do each come in a variety of colors and sizes, but there are numerous different shapes to choose from as well, such as snowflakes, leaves and flowers. The specialty eyelet shapes usually require an ⅛" (3mm) hole. When selecting eyelets or brads, one thing to consider is the depth of the shaft that your papercraft will require. Some eyelets will not be long enough to go through a layer of cardstock and corrugated paper. Before you go out shopping, measure the depth of your project or take a sample along with you to the store.

TIP

When making a template for use in creating multiples of any papercraft, take the time to make sure all of the edges are straight or smooth and, if appropriate, the corners are 90° angles. The more time you take to make a perfect template, the fewer problems you'll encounter when it comes time to assemble your projects.

GIFT CANDLE

You'll be amazed by the generous, helpful spirit of friends and family as they assist you with wedding day preparations. Thank each one of your helpers in a special way with this gift candle, bearing a personalized note of gratitude from the bride and groom.

what you will
need

- burgundy pillar candle, 6" (15cm) tall and 3" (8cm) in diameter
- 26" × 40" (66cm × 102cm) burgundy corrugated paper
- 8½" × 11" (22cm × 28cm) plum leaf paper
- 30" (76cm) burgundy raffia
- 3" (8cm) burgundy skeleton leaf
- ⅛" (3mm) hole punch
- scissors
- ruler
- pencil
- double-sided tape
- white craft glue

1 Create a document for a 2" (5cm) square. Center the text, and start the words ¼" (6mm) down from the top of the label. The font used here was Papyrus at 12pt. Print the tag label on the leaf paper, and trim the label to 2" (5cm) square.

2 Cut a 2¼" (6cm) square from the corrugated paper. With double-sided tape stick the printed label onto the corrugated tag. Punch a hole in the top left corner of the tag.

3 Cut a strip of burgundy corrugated paper to 4" × 9½" (10cm × 24cm) and a strip of leaf paper to 2½" × 11" (6cm × 28cm). Adjust these

lengths as necessary if your candle is not 3" (8cm) in diameter. The corrugated paper should go around the candle, but the two ends should not quite meet. The leaf paper should be 1½" (4cm) longer than the corrugated piece.

4 Run a strip of double-sided tape along one of the 4" (10cm) ends of the leaf paper. Center the leaf paper over the corrugated paper, and attach the taped end to one end of the corrugated paper. The other end of the leaf paper will extend 1½" (4cm) past the end of the corrugated paper.

5 Place craft glue onto the back of the 1½"

(4cm) of leaf paper that extends beyond the corrugated paper. Wrap the papers tightly around the center of the candle, and secure the glued tab.

6 Put a very small strip of double-sided tape on the center of the burgundy leaf. Stick the leaf onto the middle of the paper band to mark the front of the candle.

7 Wrap the raffia around the candle twice so the two ends meet at the leaf. Slip the tag onto the raffia and tie the raffia into a bow.

POCKET BOOKMARK

Choose a quote or verse that is particularly meaningful to you, then share it with your guests on this pocket bookmark. The finished product is more than just a bookmark — it is a lovely little work of art that will serve as a cherished reminder of your day.

what you will need

- 26" × 40" (66cm × 102cm) burgundy corrugated paper
- 12" (30cm) square salmon leaf text-weight paper
- 8½" × 11" (22cm × 28cm) off-white cardstock
- 8½" × 11" (22cm × 28cm) burgundy cardstock
- 16" (41cm) burgundy raffia
- six ⅛" (3mm) antique brass eyelets

- ⅛" (3mm) hole punch
- eyelet setter
- hammer
- cutting mat
- scissors
- ruler
- pencil
- double-sided tape

1 Create a document for a 1½" × 6½" (4cm × 17cm) bookmark. Begin the words 1" (3cm) from the top. Here, the font Papyrus was used at 24pt for the word *love* and 16pt for the rest of the verse. Print the verse on the salmon leaf paper, and trim to size.

2 Cut the burgundy cardstock to 1¾" × 6¾" (4.5cm × 17.5cm) and cut the off-white cardstock to 2¼" × 7¼" (6cm × 18cm). Put a small strip of double-sided tape on the back of the printed leaf paper and center it onto the burgundy paper. Then tape the burgundy paper to the off-white paper.

3 Measure 1" (3cm) from the top of the bookmark, and mark the center of the bookmark between the two outer edges with a pencil. Punch a hole at the mark. Put an eyelet into the hole and set it (see Setting Eyelets, page 118). Do the same 1" (3cm) from the bottom.

4 Cut two 8" (20cm) lengths of the raffia. Put the two lengths of raffia together and fold them in half to form a loop. Stick the loop through the eyelet at the top of the bookmark

from front to back. Pull the loop through 2" (5cm) to 3" (8cm). Place the ends of the raffia through the loop and gently pull the ends until the loop is snug around the top of the bookmark. Trim the ends even.

5 Cut a piece of the burgundy corrugated paper to 3¾" × 8" (10cm × 20cm). The corrugation lines should run parallel to the 8" (20cm) length. Cut another piece of the burgundy corrugated paper to 3¾" × 3½" (10cm × 9cm). The corrugation lines should run parallel with the 3¾" (10cm) length.

6 Place the 3¾" × 3½" (10cm × 9cm) piece on the end of the 3¾" × 8" (10cm × 20cm) piece. Line up the corners, and make sure the bottom edges are aligned. Punch a hole in each corner of the pocket about an ⅛" (3mm) from each edges. Set an eyelet in each hole. Place the bookmark into the pocket.

Janice Matilda Pupeza
and
Mark Jethrow Carroll
together with their parents
request your presence at their wedding
on Saturday, the eighteenth of October
Two thousand and three
at eleven o'clock in the morning
First Alliance Church
20314 County Road 14
Big Lake, Minnesota
Reception following in Fellowship Hall

Thank you for sharing
our day with u...
Janice and Mark

The favor of your reply is req...
by the third of October

Name _____

_____ Number of guests
...ing

a change of SEASON

What could be a more beautiful backdrop for your wedding than this one that Mother Nature herself provides? With its rich harvest colors, autumn's palette is perfect for a warm, comfortable wedding celebration.

The papercrafts in this set are fitting for a casual event on a crisp sunny autumn afternoon or for an evening affair that is a bit more formal. To represent the season, a single leaf is the dominant design element throughout the projects. If you want to add a special touch, choose a leaf from a tree that is native to your home region or the location of the wedding.

The copper tones of the leaf invitation extend a warm welcome to your guests. The table decorations and the guest book set, both bearing the leaf motif, are wonderful seasonal accents. For a special wedding keepsake, your guests will cherish the fall votive candle favors, while you can enjoy a gift to yourself — the custom-made accordion file for all your wedding-related materials and mementos.

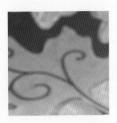

INVITATION • GUEST BOOK • BEADED PEN • CANDLE FAVOR • TABLE CONFETTI • KEEPSAKE FILE

INVITATION

*Introduce the fall theme of your wedding by sending out this gorgeous invitation,
stamped with a leaf design and treated with a variety of colored embossing powders.
Tailor the design to your taste by selecting whatever leaf stamp strikes your fancy.*

Janice Matilda Pupeza
and
Mark Jethrow Carroll
together with their parents
request your presence at their wedding
on Saturday, the eighteenth of October
Two thousand and three
at eleven o'clock in the morning
First Alliance Church
20314 County Road 14
Big Lake, Minnesota
Reception following in Fellowship Hall

what you will need

- 8½" × 11" (22cm × 28cm) cream cardstock, 2 sheets
- 8½" × 11" (22cm × 28cm) copper metallic cardstock
- 8½" × 11" (22cm × 28cm) clear translucent vellum
- 5½" (14cm) square envelope
- no. 4 envelope
- 7" (18cm) of ⅝" (2cm) copper double-faced satin ribbon
- small gold maple leaf charm
- gold "O" ring
- bronze metallic ink pad
- large double oak leaf stamp (Stamp Francisco)
- small double oak leaf stamp (Stamp Francisco)
- various fall-colored embossing powders
- scissors
- ruler
- pencil
- ⅛" (3mm) hole punch
- heat gun
- small spoon
- paintbrush
- double-sided tape

The favor of your reply is requested
by the third of October

Name _____

_____ Number of guests attending

1 Create a document that is 5" (13cm) square. Begin the text 1⅜" (3cm) from the top and center the text. Here, the font Pristina was used at 16pt. Print the invitation wording onto the vellum, and trim to size.

2 Create a 3½" × 5" (9cm × 13cm) document for a card, centering the text (Pristina at 16pt). Print the response card on the cream card-stock, and trim to size.

3 Cut the copper paper to a 5¼" (13cm) square. Cut the second sheet of cream card-stock to a 5" (13cm) square.

4 To prepare your work area for stamping, set out a sheet of scrap paper at least 5½" × 8½" (14cm × 22cm) for each color of powder. Take the lids off all the embossing powder containers so that you can use them quickly before the ink dries. Ink the smaller oak leaf stamp and stamp it onto the response card. Spoon one of the embossing powders over a small portion of the leaves. Tap the excess powder off onto one of the scrap pieces of paper, taking care to keep the powder off the other inked portion of the leaves. Quickly repeat this process (using a different piece of scrap paper for each powder

color) until you have used all of the powders randomly on the inked image. Return the excess of each color of powder to its own container when you're done. Brush any excess powder off the paper with the paintbrush.

5 With the heat gun, heat the powdered area until the powders melt to a shiny, smooth finish. Set the response card aside to cool.

6 Stamp the large oak leaf stamp onto the center of the 5" (13cm) square piece of cream cardstock. Apply and heat embossing powders as you did in steps 4 and 5.

7 Adhere the 5" (13cm) cream square card-stock onto the center of the copper paper square with double-sided tape.

8 Measure ½" (1cm) from the top of the printed vellum piece. Make a mark 2" (5cm) from the left side and another mark 2" (5cm) from the right side.

9 Line up the printed vellum over the cream side of the layered card from step 7. Punch holes at the marks on the vellum, punching through the vellum and the card.

10 Put the leaf charm onto the "O"ring.

11 Thread one end of the ribbon through the

left hole from the front of the invitation to the back, leaving a 1½" (4cm) to 2" (5cm) tail. Thread the same end of the ribbon through the other hole to the front of the invitation. Pull the ribbon taut, but do not change the length of the tail. Slide the "O"ring with the charm all the way to the end of the ribbon at the right hole, charm facing out. Thread that end of ribbon back through the left hole to the back of the invitation. Pull the ribbon enough so that the center section of the ribbon on the front of the invitation is flat and not too loose. Thread that same end of the ribbon through the right hole to the front of the invitation, to make the other tail. Trim the ends of the ribbon. If you have a difficult time getting the ribbon through the holes, use some type of pointed instrument to help guide the ribbon, but make sure it does not mar the ribbon.

12 This invitation fits in a 5½" (14cm) square envelope. If you wish, stamp and emboss the small leaf stamp on the bottom right corner and the back flap of the envelope. The response card fits into a no. 4 envelope.

Variation Idea

An alternative card for this theme is this tall oak leaf card. Instead of stamping and embossing the leaves, use a leaf-shaped paper punch to punch the leaves out of fall-colored decorative paper. Use a glue stick to glue the leaves onto cream cardstock, 3½" × 8½" (9cm × 22cm). Layer the cream cardstock onto bronze cardstock cut to 3¾" × 8¾" (10cm × 22cm) then copper cardstock cut to 4" × 9¼" (10cm × 24cm), with double-sided tape. Create a 3½" × 8½" (9cm × 22cm) document, beginning the text 1⅜" (3cm) from the top. Print the invitation onto the vellum. Secure it to the layered card with eyelets placed ¾" (2cm) from the top and bottom of the card. This card fits into a no. 10 envelope.

GUEST BOOK

The colors and textures of autumn make this guest book warm, sumptuous and inviting. It is the perfect record of those guests who made your day special!

- 12" (30cm) square soft rust embossed suede paper, 2 sheets
- 8½" × 11" (22cm × 28cm) copper cardstock, 2 sheets
- 8½" × 11" (22cm × 28cm) cream cardstock
- 8½" × 11" (22cm × 28cm) cream vellum
- 8½" × 11" (22cm × 28cm) cream text-weight paper, 10-12 sheets

- 36" (91cm) of ⅝" (2cm) orange wired ribbon
- bronze metallic ink pad
- leaf stamp (Magenta)
- various fall-colored embossing powders
- scissors
- ruler

- pencil
- bone folder
- ¼" (6mm) hole punch
- small spoon
- paintbrush
- heat gun
- large needle

- clamps
- scrap piece of mat board
- decorative corner scissors
- corner punch
- glue stick
- craft glue

1 Cut the suede paper and the copper cardstock to 6" × 9" (15cm × 23cm) to get two sheets of each. With a glue stick, glue one copper piece to the back of each suede cover piece. Burnish well with the bone folder to make a strong bond.

2 Cut the text-weight sheets in half to get twenty to thirty 5½" × 8½" (14cm × 22cm) pages. Punch three holes in the end of each page. To do this by hand, make a template with one page. Punch the outer holes at least 1" (3cm) from each edge and center the third hole between the first two.

3 Wrap the pages of the book tightly with a scrap piece of paper to hold them even and secure, leaving the holes exposed. Brush a thin layer of white craft glue across the paper ends. Let dry completely. This creates a pad of pages that won't move out of place as you cover them.

4 Using a punched page as a template, punch holes in the cover pieces.

5 Score a fold line on the inside of the front cover, 1¼" (3cm) from the hole-punched edge,
using a bone folder and a ruler. This enables the book to open smoothly.

6 Place the pages between the covers, making sure all the holes line up. Place scrap pieces of mat board on the back and front cover to prevent the covers from being marred, and use the clamps to hold the book together.

7 Thread a large needle with the ribbon. Leaving a 7" (18cm) tail, push the needle and ribbon down through the center hole, going from the front to the back. Push the needle up through the bottom hole, bring the ribbon around the outside edge of the book, and push the needle up through the same hole. (Push the ribbon aside as you repeatedly go through the holes so that you don't pierce it. Be careful not to twist the ribbon as you bind the book.) Wrap the ribbon around the bottom edge of the book, and push the needle back up through the same hole again. Push the needle down through the center hole, and repeat the process with the top hole. Bring the ribbon that is hanging out of the back around to the
front of the book and tie a shoestring bow with the first tail (see Shoestring Bow, page120).

8 Trim the ribbon ends and add a drop of craft glue to secure the knot.

9 Cut a piece of copper cardstock to 4¼" × 5½" (11cm × 14cm). Round the corners with corner scissors, and use a corner punch to make slits to hold the label.

10 Create a document for a label that is 3⅝" × 4⅞" (9cm × 12cm). Start the text 1" (3cm) from the top and center the text. Print the label onto the vellum, and trim to size.

11 Trim the cream cardstock to 3⅝" × 4⅞" (9cm × 12cm). Ink and stamp the leaf stamp. Emboss the leaf as described in steps 4 and 5 on page 73.

12 Place the vellum over the stamped cardstock and slide the two pieces into the slits in the copper cardstock. Glue the label to the cover with a glue stick.

BEADED PEN

What better way to complete the elegant look of your guest book than with a matching pen? To make it, discard the plastic end at the top of a round-barreled pen. Cut a piece of suede paper to 1" × 5" (3cm × 13cm). With a paintbrush, spread a thin coat of white craft glue onto the back of the strip of paper. Wrap the paper around the pen. Make the decorative top to the pen by curling 4" (10cm) of copper wire into a spiral. String beads on the wire beneath the spiral. Finish with a bead that will fit into the barrel of the pen. Glue the bead and wire into the barrel. Let dry completely.

CANDLE COLOR

The color of the candles you choose can reflect the tone and overall sentiment of your wedding. While you may choose a candle based solely on a thematic color scheme, consider the meaning of the color you choose. You might even print a description of the symbolic meaning on the printed band that surrounds the candle.

Blue: Wisdom, harmony, peace and inner light

Brown: Earth energy, material wealth, family and stability

Gold: Prosperity, wealth, healing and understanding

Green: Success, good luck, harmony and rejuvenation

Orange: Stamina, adaptability, balance and mental agility

Pink: Emotions from the heart, new beginnings and hope

Purple: Power, success, idealism and independence

Red: Courage, passion, respect and strength

White: Protection, purity, unity, positive energy and peace

Yellow: Charm, confidence, healing, joy and attraction

CANDLE FAVOR

Transform ordinary votive candles into very special treasures, simply by adding decorative fibers and elegant acorn charms. In addition to wonderful memories, your guests will also have this charming keepsake to take home with them!

what you will need

- votive candle, 3" (8cm) tall and 2" (5cm) in diameter
- 8½" × 11" (22cm × 28cm) cream parchment paper
- 18" (46cm) of fall-colored fibers
- large antique gold acorn charm
- small antique gold acorn charm
- gold "O" ring
- scissors
- ruler
- pencil
- double-sided tape

1 Create a document for a 2½" × 9" (6cm × 23cm) band. Begin the text ½" (1cm) from the top of the paper and center the text, leaving a 1" (3cm) space in the center for the fibers. Here, the font Pristina was used at 16pt. Print the band on the parchment paper, and trim to size.

2 Wrap the band around the votive, and secure the ends with double-sided tape. Make sure the band is tight so that it won't slip off of the candle.

3 Wrap the fibers around the candle twice, ending at the front of the candle. Add the acorn charms to the "O" ring, slip the "O" ring on the fibers and tie a knot. Trim the fiber ends if necessary.

TABLE CONFETTI

Constructed from paper and decorated with a gold paint pen, these table accents easily bring the beauty of the autumn season indoors. Scatter the leaves on tables or hang them from fishing line to fill your reception site with the festive spirit of fall.

what you will need

- cardstock in fall colors
- vellum in fall colors
- scissors
- pencil
- gold paint pen
- leaf patterns (page 123)

1 Enlarge the patterns on page 123 as desired, and trace the patterns onto fall-colored cardstock and vellum. Cut out the shapes.

2 With the gold paint pen, add fanciful veins to the front and back of the leaves.

TIP

If you have a shape-cutting tool, try purchasing a leaf template to fit your system. It will make quick work of creating these festive table decorations.

KEEPSAKE FILE

This beautiful file makes wedding organization a pleasure.
Use it before the wedding to keep papers, samples and contracts in one
place. Use it afterwards to hold cards, mementos and photographs.

what you will
need

- accordion file with flap
- 12" (30cm) square leaf paper, 4 sheets
- 46" (117cm) of ⅝" (2cm) wide copper double-faced satin ribbon

- paper plate
- small paint roller
- paintbrush
- craft knife

- scissors
- ruler
- pencil
- white craft glue

1 Measure from the bottom of the front flap of the file to the seam at the back, then add 1" (3cm). Take separate measurements for the inside of the flap; the front of the folder; and the back of the folder.

2 With the ruler and craft knife, cut the oak leaf paper for each of the four sections according to your measurements.

3 Put scrap paper down to protect your work area, and have a damp cloth nearby to wipe glue off your hands as needed. Pour ¼ cup to ½ cup (59ml to 118ml) glue onto a paper plate. Roll the paint roller in the glue, to cover the roller with glue.

4 Roll an even layer of glue onto the front section of the folder. Make sure the glue goes all the way to the edges. Carefully lay the cut piece of paper onto the glued section. The paper will be hard to move after it is in place, so be as exact as possible when laying it on. When it is in place, smooth the paper to get rid of any bubbles. Secure the edges, putting a little glue on the brush and brushing it where needed.

5 Cover the roller in glue again, then repeat the process in step 4 on the back of the file.

6 Next, repeat step 4 to glue the front flap section in place. Put the 1" (3cm) overlap at the back of the file.

7 To attach the ribbon, measure 1" (3cm) in from the edge of the flap, and center the mark between the outside edges. With the craft knife, make a slit here that is a little wider than the ribbon, about ¾" (2cm).

8 With scissors, cut the ribbon to a 12" (30cm) length piece and a 34" (86cm) piece. Place the end of the longer ribbon through the front of the slit. Pull 1" (3cm) of the ribbon through the slit. This ribbon will go up over the top of the file, down the back and up from the bottom, then tie to the other ribbon. Glue the 1" (3cm) end of the ribbon on the inside of the flap, pointed toward the top of the file. Let dry.

9 Place the end of the other ribbon through the front of the slit. Pull 1" (3cm) of the ribbon through the slit. Glue the end of the ribbon to the inside of the flap, and pointed toward the edge of the flap. Let dry.

10 Roll glue on the inside flap of the file and attach the last section of leaf paper. Press it smooth, and let dry.

CUTTING WITH A CRAFT KNIFE

A craft knife is an all-purpose cutting knife, producing straight, sharp edges. Here are a few tips that will make cutting with a craft knife a little easier.

- Use the grid markings on your cutting mat for measuring and lining up the paper while cutting. You won't need to make as many marks on your paper and your corners will be perfectly square.

- When cutting with your metal ruler, hold the ruler down firmly with your non-cutting hand, and keep that hand on the ruler until you've completed the cut. You may need to make several cutting strokes to cut through many layers of paper or heavy card.

- Hold the knife like a pen, with your index finger (it's your strongest) on top of the handle. Cleaner cuts can be made by exerting downward pressure on the blade while cutting.

- Make sure the blade is held at a constant, low angle to the paper, and make strong, one-motion cuts toward you. Don't press really hard or you will rip the paper.

- Always measure twice and cut once.

wishes of GOOD FORTUNE

This theme, inspired by a traditional Chinese wedding ceremony, reflects the growing popularity of the Asian aesthetic in Western culture. The bold colors and exciting design appeal to couples of all cultural backgrounds!

Many of the projects resonate with age-old Chinese symbolism. The use of red, the traditional color of weddings in China, symbolizes love, joy and prosperity. The coin tassel invites wealth and good fortune, a common wish for any newlywed couple. The character used on the invitation and the seal is the Chinese character for love, and the character used on the wedding program stands for double happiness.

These papercrafts breathe life into any wedding. The invitation only hints at the lively favors to follow—a gorgeous wedding program, a glowing paper lantern, a graceful origami swan and a favor box suitable for any small treat. Your guests will take pleasure in the truly exuberant spirit of your celebration!

INVITATION · PROGRAM · LUMINARY · BOX FAVOR · CHOPSTICK WRAP · SWAN CENTERPIECE

INVITATION

When the tassel is removed from the dual-button closure, the two front flaps of this invitation open like French doors. With the appealing design and eye-catching colors, who will be able to resist such a dramatic wedding invitation?

what you will need

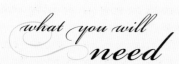

- 8½" × 11" (22cm × 28cm) red flecked cardstock, 2 sheets
- 8½" × 11" (22cm × 28cm) black flecked cardstock
- 8½" × 11" (22cm × 28cm) red and gold decorative paper
- 8½" × 11" (22cm × 28cm) gold metallic cardstock

- A-7 envelope
- 1½" (4cm) gold tassel
- two ⅛" (3mm) gold eyelets
- black pigment ink pad
- Chinese love character rubber stamp (Inkadinkado)
- scissors

- ruler
- pencil
- bone folder
- ⅛" (3mm) hole punch
- 1" (3cm) circle punch
- ½" (1cm) circle punch
- eyelet setter

- hammer
- cutting mat
- double-sided tape
- glue stick

1 Cut the black cardstock to 7" × 10⅛" (18cm × 26cm). With a ruler and pencil, measure and mark 2⅝" (7cm) in from the left side of the paper. Score along this line with the ruler and a bone folder. Fold the flap in toward the center of the paper.

2 Measure 2½" (6cm) from the right side of the paper. Use the ruler and bole folder to score along this line, then fold the flap in toward the other flap. The two flaps should touch each other with no gap between them.

3 Cut four 1" × 7" (3cm × 18cm) strips from the red and gold decorative paper. Use double-sided tape to adhere one strip to the left flap, placing the strip ¼" (6mm) in from the edge. Repeat on the right flap. Set the remaining two strips of paper aside.

4 Punch two 1" (3cm) circles out of the scrap black cardstock and two ½" (1cm) circles from the gold cardstock. Put one gold circle onto the center of one black circle and punch with the ⅛" (3mm) hole punch. Repeat with the other set of circles.

5 On the left flap, measure and mark 3½" (9cm) down from the top in the center of the decorative strip. Punch a ⅛" (3mm) hole on the mark through just the flap, not the entire card. Repeat on the right flap.

6 Put an eyelet through one set of circles and place it through the hole on the left flap. Set the eyelet (see Setting Eyelets, page 118). Repeat on the right flap.

7 Using the glue stick, adhere one of the remaining strips of decorative paper onto the inside of the left flap ¼" (6mm) in from the edge of the flap. This will conceal the back of the set eyelet. Repeat on the right flap.

8 Create a document that is 4⅞" × 7" (12cm × 18cm). Begin the text 2" (5cm) from the top of the paper, and center the text. The font used here is Hansa bold at 16pt. Print the invitation on the red cardstock, and trim to 4⅞" × 7" (12cm × 18cm). Ink and stamp the Chinese love character stamp on the invitation, center-ing it between the top of the card and the lettering. Also stamp the back flap of an A-7 envelope. Allow the ink to dry.

9 Prepare the reply postcard in the same way, but create a document for a 3½" × 5" (9cmx 13cm) card. Begin the words 1¾" (4cm) from the top of the postcard. Use the same paper in the same font and point size as the invitation. Print the postcard, and trim it to size. Stamp the Chinese love character between the top of the card and the lettering. Allow the ink to dry.

10 To assemble, place the reply postcard (return address down) in the gatefold first, and then the invitation. Close the flaps and put the tassel around the two buttons so the tassel hangs below the buttons.

PROGRAM

This program is held together by an old Asian bookbinding technique called stab binding. On the program cover is the Chinese symbol for double happiness: two happiness characters placed side by side to represent the wish for newlywed bliss.

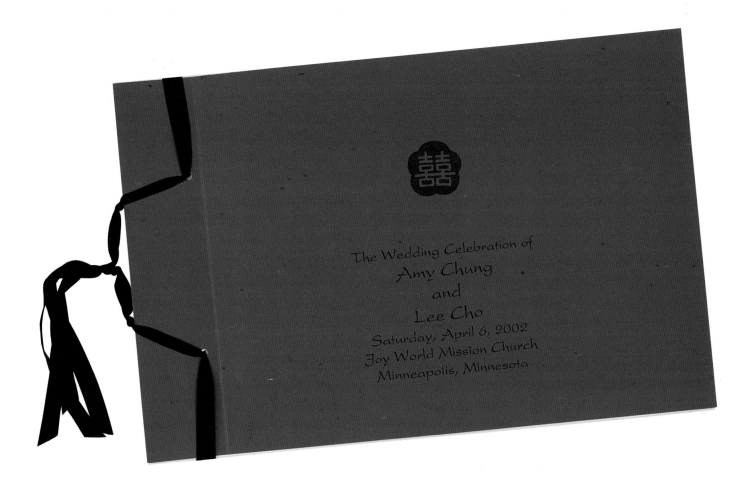

The Wedding Celebration of
Amy Chung
and
Lee Cho
Saturday, April 6, 2002
Joy World Mission Church
Minneapolis, Minnesota

what you will need

- 8½" × 11" (22cm × 28cm) red flecked cardstock
- 8½" × 11" (22cm × 28cm) white flecked text-weight paper
- 32" (81cm) of ¼" (6mm) black silk ribbon
- black ink pad
- double happiness seal stamp (Inkadinkado)

- scissors
- ruler
- pencil
- bone folder
- ⅛" (3mm) hole punch
- binder clips
- large blunt-end needle

1 Cut the red cardstock in half to make two 5½" × 8½" (14cm × 22cm) pieces for the front and back covers of the book. Print the program cover wording on one piece, starting 2¾" (7cm) from the top of the paper. Begin the top line of the text 3¼" (8cm) from the left edge. Center the subsequent lines of text below the top line. Here, the Hansa font was used at 20pt and 16pt.

2 Cut the white paper in half to make two 5½" × 8½" (14cm × 22cm) sheets. Print the wedding ceremony information on the two pages. Your spacing will depend on the amount of information you have. Begin the text 2" (5cm) from the left side of the paper.

3 On the left side of the cover, measure 1" (3cm) from the edge and 1½" (4cm) from the top and make a mark. Repeat with a second mark 1" (3cm) from the edge and 1½" (4cm) from the bottom.

4 Punch a hole at each mark. Using the cover as a template, punch the back cover and the pages. Make sure the pages are facing the correct way before punching. Stack the pages into the proper sequence.

5 Use the clips to secure the program at the top and bottom, placing the clips away from the holes.

6 Cut two 16" (41cm) lengths of black ribbon. Thread one length of ribbon through the needle. Push the needle through the top hole from the front of the program to the back. Bring the ribbon over the top of the program and push the needle back into the same hole. Be careful not to sew through the ribbon. Adjust the ribbon so the two tails are the same length. One tail should be coming out of the back of the hole; the other one, out of the front. Pull the ribbon taut, and tie the two tails into an overhand knot on the left edge of the book. Repeat for the bottom hole.

7 Tie the two pairs of tails together in an overhand knot. Trim the ends if necessary.

8 With the ruler and bone folder, mark 1¼" (3cm) from the left side of the program on the top and bottom of the front cover. Score along this line to make the cover easier to open.

9 Ink and stamp the double happiness seal stamp on the cover of the program, centering it between the top of the program and the wording. Let the ink dry.

BINDING
ALTERNATIVES

Using ribbon to bind a booklet is only one of many options, both traditional and more contemporary. Explore the use of waxed bookbinding thread, as well as decorative fibers used in needle arts. There are many colors and weights for each of these options, and you can find materials online (try www.hollanders.com or www.sewingcrafting.com), as well as at local craft and sewing stores.

LUMINARY

With these paper lanterns, you can add beautiful ambience to an evening wedding.
Use a votive candle inside a clear glass holder to illuminate the lantern, and prevent
contact with the open flame by securing the lantern to the paper mat with clear tape.

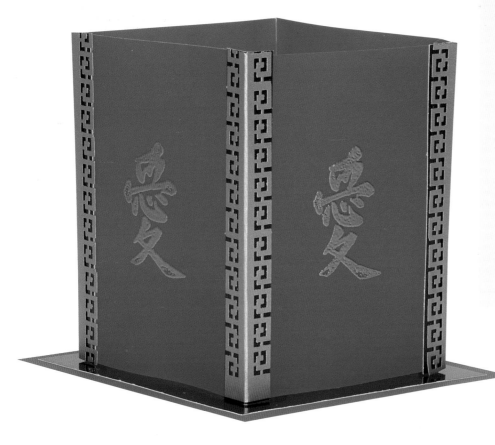

what you will
need

- 8½" × 11" (22cm × 28cm) heavyweight red vellum, 2 sheets
- 8½" × 11" (22cm × 28cm) metallic gold cardstock
- 8½" × 11" (22cm × 28cm) black glossy cardstock
- 8½" × 11" (22cm × 28cm) red cardstock
- gold pigment ink pad
- Chinese love character stamp (Inkadinkado)
- gold embossing powder
- scissors
- ruler
- pencil
- bone folder
- Greek key design border punch
- heat gun
- glue stick
- double-sided tape

1 Cut four 4" × 5" (10cm × 13cm) pieces from the red vellum. Stamp the Chinese love character in the middle of each red vellum panel with gold ink. Sprinkle each with gold embossing powder and heat with heat gun (see Thermal Embossing, page 119). Set aside.

2 Cut four 1½" × 6" (4cm × 15cm) strips from the gold cardstock. With the border punch, punch all the gold strips on both sides. Score lengthwise down the middle of the gold strips and fold each strip in half.

3 Cut four 1" × 6" (3cm × 15cm) strips from the black cardstock. Score and fold lengthwise down the middle of each.

4 Use a dabbing motion with a glue stick, to apply glue to the gold strips and adhere them to the black strips. Use the bone folder to burnish. Fold these decorative strips in half and burnish for a sharp crease.

5 To assemble the luminary, apply double-sided tape to both halves of the insides of all the decorative strips and adhere them to the

red panels. Leave the protective film on one edge until ready to use if transporting the luminaries to the reception area.

6 Trim the strips even with the tops of the red panels. To construct the mats, cut the remaining black paper to 5" (13cm) square and the red cardstock to 5½" (14cm) square. Center the black piece on the red piece and adhere it with a glue stick.

BOX FAVOR

Send your guests a special wish for wealth and good fortune by presenting them with a coin tassel in this favor box. Reproduction Chinese coins are readily available, but for about the same cost, you can purchase authentic antique coins, which have a beautiful patina.

- 8½" × 11" (22cm × 28cm) red text weight paper
- 8½" × 11" (22cm × 28cm) decorative paper or piece of Chinese newspaper
- 8½" × 11" (22cm × 28cm) black glossy cardstock
- 8½" × 11" (22cm × 28cm) gold metallic cardstock
- 6" (15cm) of ½" (1cm) wide black ribbon
- Chinese coin
- black embroidery floss
- decorative punch, Asian design
- scissors
- ruler
- pencil
- bone folder
- 5" (13cm) wide mat board
- glue stick
- double-sided tape
- white craft glue

1 Use a glue stick to glue the red paper to the decorative paper. Cut out two 4" × 4¾" (10cm × 12cm) pieces from the double-sided paper. Make a box from these two pieces (see Making a Quick Box, page 114).

2 Use double-sided tape to attach the ribbon along the top of the box and around the edges of the lid.

3 Cut a 1½" (4cm) square from the black cardstock. Cut a 1¼" (3cm) square from the gold cardstock. Punch the gold panel, and glue it onto the black panel with the glue stick.

4 Finish the box by gluing the decorative panel on the box top with glue stick.

5 To make a tassel, wrap the embroidery floss around the mat board ten times. Remove the floss from the board, and cut the bottom loops. Thread the top of the floss, still in a loop, through the hole in the coin. Thread the cut ends through the loop and pull to tighten. If desired, place a bit of craft glue on the knot in the back. Place the lucky coin tassel into the box for your guests.

CHOPSTICK WRAP

For a favor variation, try this chopstick wrap. Cut a 2" × 5" (5cm × 13cm) strip from red cardstock. Fold the strip into thirds, creating a 2" (5cm) square panel in the front. Tape the ends together in the back. For the decorative panel, follow the instructions in step 3 of the box project. Glue the decorative panel to the center of the band, then slide in the chopsticks.

CUTTING PAPER SWANS

These swans can be made any size you like. Generally, the finished swan size, measuring from tip of the beak across to the tail, will be 1" (3cm) smaller than the size of the square you start with. Because the angle of the folds can vary with this design, the sizes are approximations only.

Cut paper into a 6" (15cm) square for a 5" (13cm) swan.

Cut paper into a 5½" (14cm) square for a 4½" (11cm) swan.

Cut paper into a 5" (13cm) square for a 4" (10cm) swan.

Cut paper into a 4½" (11cm) square for a 3½" (9cm) swan.

Cut paper into a 4" (10cm) square for a 3" (8cm) swan.

Cut paper into a 3½" (9cm) square for a 2½" (6cm) swan.

Cut paper into a 3" (8cm) square for a 2" (5cm) swan.

SWAN CENTERPIECE

This simple origami swan takes much less time to create than the common crane design, yet it is no less graceful. Use these paper swans to accent your wedding décor by incorporating them into bamboo table arrangements or by placing them onto a black glossy paper mat, along with a luminary.

what you will need

- 8½" × 11" (22cm × 28cm) red text-weight paper
- 8½" × 11" (22cm × 28cm) black glossy cardstock
- 8½" × 11" (22cm × 28cm) red cardstock
- metallic gold spray paint
- slide cutter
- bone folder
- glue stick
- hot glue gun

1 Apply a thin coat of gold spray paint to one side of the red paper in a well-ventilated area, and let dry completely. Using the slide cutter, cut squares from the painted paper (see Cutting Paper Swans, page 88). Fold one square in half diagonally. Unfold the square and lay flat with either the red or gold side up. Fold the two side corners into the middle fold line. Burnish the folds with the bone folder.

2 Fold both sides toward the center, this time going about halfway to the middle fold. This does not need to be exactly measured, but make sure the bottom point is sharp and even. Burnish these folds down with the bone folder.

3 Fold the piece in half at the center fold. Burnish the fold.

4 Fold the pointed end upward to form the neck of the swan. Fold the tip of the neck piece down to form the head.

5 Cut the black cardstock to 7" × 8" (18cm × 20cm) and the red cardstock to 7½" × 8½" (19cm × 22cm). Center the black piece on the red piece and adhere them with a glue stick. You can simply set the swans on the base or use a glue gun to glue them in place.

Linda Jean Gaslin
and
Clarion Dee Holloway

October 8, 2005
Jesus People Church

Linda Jean Gaslin
and
Clarion Dee Holloway
together with their parents
Mr. and Mrs. Kenneth Gaslin
and
Mr. and Mrs. Jim Holloway
invite you to share in the joy
when they exchange marriage vows
on Saturday, the eighth of October
two thousand and five
at five o'clock in the afternoon
People Church
Avenue South
Minnesota

a formal INDULGENCE

For the couple planning a traditional, formal wedding, the fleur-de-lis theme offers timeless beauty. Often associated with royalty, the fleur-de-lis lends elegance and refinement to your special day. Its design is classic yet unique, a mark of distinction that will set your wedding apart from all others.

The papercrafts in this set reflect a taste for tradition over trend. Touches of gold, a graceful script and the fleur-de-lis emblem announce the formality of your wedding celebration. From the moment they receive your invitations, your guests will anticipate a splendid, sophisticated and stylish affair!

The repetition of the fleur-de-lis motif unifies all the components of the set while setting a regal tone. Even though the invitation, program, menu card and thank-you card are all common elements of a wedding set, there is nothing common about these papercrafts. Add the wine wrap and favor packet to set a new standard for wedding style!

INVITATION • PROGRAM • FOLD-OVER FAVOR • MENU CARD • THANK-YOU CARD • WINE WRAP

INVITATION

Formal elegance is at the heart of this folded invitation, accented by a gold fleur-de-lis and a gold embossed deckle edge. Traditionally, this style of invitation includes wedding information only on the front, while the inside is left blank.

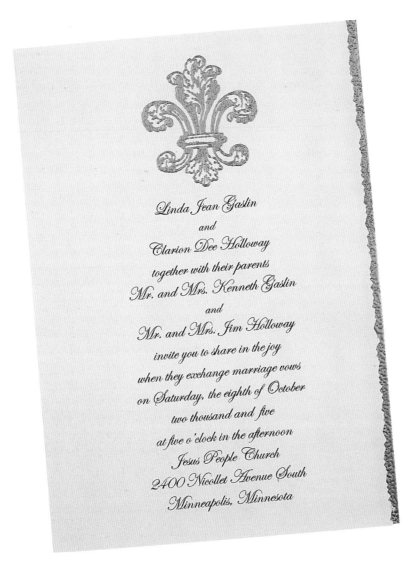

Linda Jean Gaslin
and
Clarion Dee Holloway
together with their parents
Mr. and Mrs. Kenneth Gaslin
and
Mr. and Mrs. Jim Holloway
invite you to share in the joy
when they exchange marriage vows
on Saturday, the eighth of October
two thousand and five
at five o'clock in the afternoon
Jesus People Church
2400 Nicollet Avenue South
Minneapolis, Minnesota

what you will need

- 8½" × 11" (22cm × 28cm) cream cardstock
- A-7 envelope
- gold metallic ink pad
- small fleur-de-lis stamp (Stamp Francisco)
- gold embossing powder
- scissors
- ruler
- pencil
- bone folder
- deckle-edged scissors
- heat gun

1 Create a 7" × 10" (18cm × 25cm) document. Start the printing 2¼" (6cm) from the top and center the text onto the right half. Print the wording onto the cardstock. Here, the font Edwardian Script ITC was used in 18pt.

2 Trim the printed cardstock to 7" × 10" (18cm × 25cm). Fold the invitation in half to 5" × 7" (13cm × 18cm) using a bone folder.

3 Cut a ⅛" (3mm) strip off the right side of the front of the invitation with the deckle-edged scissors. This will make the front of the invitation ⅛" (3mm) narrower than the back.

4 Place an 8½" × 11" (22cm × 28cm) scrap of paper onto your work surface, then open the card so it is flat with the front side down. Use the ink pad to smear ink onto the right edge of the paper.

5 Sprinkle embossing powder over the inked area on the card. Gently tap off the excess powder from the card onto the scrap paper.

6 Pour excess powder back into its container. Heat the powdered area with the heat gun. Let the card cool. Leave the scrap paper on the work surface for more embossing that will be done in the next step.

7 Ink the rubber stamp and stamp the front of the invitation, centering the fleur-de-lis between the top of the card and the wording. Sprinkle embossing powder over the inked area. Gently tap off the excess powder from the card onto the scrap paper. Heat the powdered area on the card. Let the card cool. Pour the excess powder back into its container. This invitation fits into an A-7 envelope.

PROGRAM

This classic wedding program echoes the traditional format and gold embellishment of the invitation. With a sense of style and an air of sophistication, it provides all the details of the wedding ceremony.

what you will need

- 8½" × 11" (22cm × 28cm) cream cardstock
- 8½" × 11" (22cm × 28cm) gold metallic vellum
- ecru tassel, with a suspension cord of 11" (28cm)
- gold metallic ink pad
- small fleur-de-lis stamp (Stampa Rosa)
- gold embossing powder
- scissors
- ruler
- pencil
- bone folder
- deckle-edged scissors
- heating gun

1 Create a document for an 8½" × 11" (22cm × 28cm) piece folded in half to 8½" × 5½" (22cm × 14cm). Start the wording 5⅛" (13cm) from the top of what will be the front panel of the program, centering the text. The font Edwardian Script ITC at 26pt was used here. Print the wording onto the cream cardstock. After the printing is dry, fold the program in half with a bone folder.

2 Using the deckle-edged scissors, cut a ⅛" (3mm) strip off the right side of the front cover. This will make the front of the program

cover ⅛" (3mm) narrower than the back.

3 Place a piece of scrap paper on your work surface. Ink the rubber stamp and stamp the front of the program, centering the fleur-de-lis between the top of the program and the wording. Sprinkle embossing powder over the inked area, and tap off the excess onto the scrap paper. Pour the excess powder back into its container, then heat with the heating gun and let the program cool.

4 Create a document with two 8½" × 5½" (22cm × 14cm) columns. Start the wording ⅞"

(2cm) from the top, using the same font at 18pt. Print the wording onto the gold paper. After the printing is dry, fold in half with the bone folder so the printing is on the inside.

5 Place the printed and folded gold paper inside the printed cover. Slip the program through the loop section of the tassel so the cording is on the fold line of the two sheets of paper. Pull the tassel down so the top of the loop is on the top of the program. Make a knot with the cording at the bottom of the program so the tassel stays in place.

FOLD-OVER FAVOR

*The custom of giving candied almonds, also called Jordan almonds or Italian confetti,
as wedding favors may date back to the ancient Romans, who showered newlyweds
with almonds as a symbol of fertility. Today at weddings, five almonds are traditionally
given to each guest to symbolize health, happiness, wealth, fertility and long life.*

what you will need

- 12" (30cm) square cream cardstock
- 8½" × 11" (22cm × 28cm) gold metallic text-weight paper
- 3¼" × 8½" (8cm × 22cm) cellophane bag
- candied almonds or gold wrapped candies
- 18" (46cm) of ¼" (6mm) gold ribbon
- gold metallic ink pad
- fleur-de-lis stamp (Stamp Francisco) (or use template to carve your own, page 123)
- gold embossing powder
- heat gun
- set of white hook-and-loop fastener dots
- scissors
- ruler
- pencil
- bone folder
- decorative corner scissors
- stapler
- craft glue
- glue stick
- glue gun

1 Cut the cardstock to 3½" × 12" (9cm × 30cm). Use the bone folder and ruler to score fold lines at 5" (13cm), 5½" (14cm) and 10½" (27cm) from one short end. Fold along the scored lines and burnish the folds with the bone folder.

2 Cut the corners of the top flap with the decorative corner scissors.

3 Accent the edges of these decorative corners by patting the edges on the ink pad.

4 Stamp the fleur-de-lis onto a scrap piece of cardstock using gold ink. Emboss the image with gold embossing powder and the heat gun. When cool, cut around the stamped image with scissors.

5 Cut a 1¾" × 2¾" (4cm × 7cm) piece from the gold paper. Layer the stamped piece of cardstock onto the gold paper and glue them

together with the glue stick. Set aside.

6 Place the almonds or other favor into the cellophane bag and staple it into the inside of the folded cardstock at the top fold, making sure the staple is in the back.

7 Fold up the front of the package and fold down the top flap.

8 Wrap a piece of ribbon vertically around the package. Use the glue gun to secure the ribbon in a few spots.

9 Attach the hook-and-loop fastener dots to create the package closure. (The dots also cover the ends of the ribbon.) Accent the front of the top flap by gluing on a separate gold shoestring bow (see Shoestring Bow, page 120) with craft glue. Use the glue stick to attach the gold panel to the front of the favor.

Variation Idea

The process for making the package shown at the above left varies just slightly from the steps listed to the left. The bow on the flap was replaced with an elegant gold polymer clay seal stamped with a small fleur-de-lis (see Making Polymer Clay Seals, page 116). The edges were embossed with gold embossing powder, and the paper with the embossed fleur-de-lis was trimmed to 1½" × 2½" (4cm × 6cm) and then layered onto gold paper. Simply elegant!

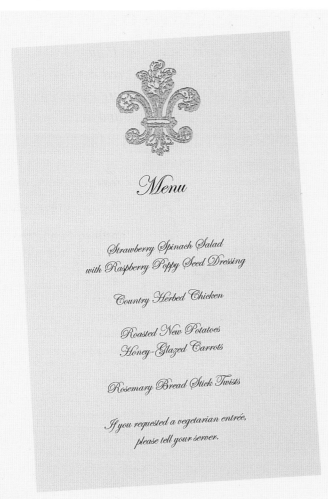

Menu

Strawberry Spinach Salad
with Raspberry Poppy Seed Dressing

Country Herbed Chicken

Roasted New Potatoes
Honey-Glazed Carrots

Rosemary Bread Stick Twists

If you requested a vegetarian entrée,
please tell your server.

MENU CARD

The menu card follows the design concept in the other pieces of the set by incorporating a larger fleur-de-lis stamped image. Print the wording on 5½" × 8½" (14cm × 22cm) cardstock, and begin the words 2½" (6cm) from the top of the paper. The font Edwardian Script ITC at 36pt was used here for the title; 20pt was used for the listing of menu items. Trim the top and bottom of the menu card with the deckle-edged scissors. Stamp the fleur-de-lis in gold ink, centering it between the top of the card and the text. Sprinkle the image with gold embossing powder, tap off the excess, and then heat with the heat gun. If you wish, make matching place cards for the reception tables, stamping and embossing a small fleur-de-lis on the left side of the card.

THANK-YOU CARD

The thank-you card uses the same stamped image and embossing technique for the deckled edge that was used for the invitation. To make this card, cut an 8½" × 11" (22cm × 28cm) piece of cream cardstock in half to 5½" × 8½" (14cm × 22cm). Score the center with a bone folder and fold the card in half. Trim the right side of the front of the card with the deckle-edged scissors. Smear the gold ink pad on the right edge of the inside of the card, like you did for the invitation (see page 92). Sprinkle the ink with embossing powder, tap off the excess, and heat to emboss. Stamp a fleur-de-lis stamp in the center of the card, and emboss the image with gold embossing powder. This card fits into a size A-2 envelope for mailing.

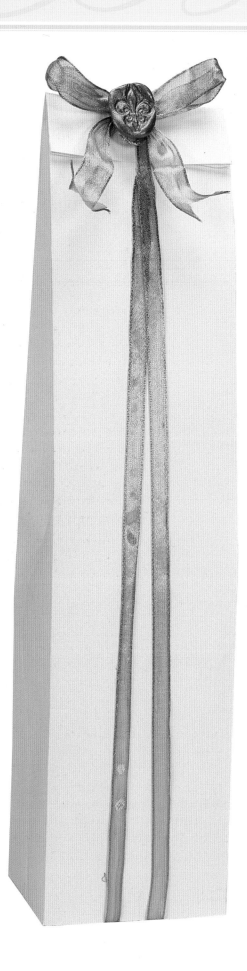

WINE WRAP

If, as the saying goes, "presentation is everything," then any bottle of wine presented in this wine wrap is sure to impress. Use the wrap for wine served at the wedding reception or for bottles of wine given to friends and family as tokens of appreciation.

what you will need

- 14" × 18" (36cm × 46cm) white ridged cover-weight paper
- 3" × 3¼" (8cm × 8cm) matboard
- 4½" (11cm) square matboard (optional, for a tassel)
- wine bottle
- stamped polymer clay seal (see page 116)
- 72" (2m) of ¼" (6mm) wide gold wired ribbon
- 24" (61cm) of ⅝" (2cm) wide gold wired ribbon
- 54" (137cm) of gold embroidery floss (optional, for a tassel)
- 12" (30cm) of gold cord (optional, for a tassel)
- stapler
- scissors
- ruler
- pencil
- bone folder
- double-sided tape
- white craft glue
- glue gun
- wine wrap pattern (on page 124)

TIP

When making your own seals of wax or polymer clay, consider stamping on the seal with a rubber stamp or metal seal to add a special touch of elegance. To prevent the wax or clay from sticking to the image, press the stamp onto a clear embossing stamp pad first. You can also press the stamp into a colored pigment ink pad to create a contrasting image in the wax or clay.

1 Using the wine wrap pattern, trim off the excess pieces of the white paper as shown. With a pencil and a ruler, measure and score all the lines that are shown. Prefold along all of the lines, folding the ones marked with a "V" (valley) with the point down, and the ones marked with an "M" (mountain) with the point up.

2 Place double-sided tape along the ½" (1cm) wide edge, on the front of the paper. Bring the opposite edge around and seal the edge of the paper right up to the V fold at the taped strip. Press the wrap flat, with the two opposite ends folded inward.

3 At the bottom of the wrap, fold in the two opposite sides that are at the front and back of the wrap, forming two pointed flaps on the alternate sides. Using craft glue under these pointed flaps, glue them down, placing your hand inside the wrap to apply opposing pressure. Glue the 3" × 3¼" (8cm × 8cm) piece of matboard into the bottom for added security.

4 Place the wine bottle into the wrap, and fold over the top flap, securing it closed with double-sided tape.

5 Beginning at the top front of the bag, wrap the ¼" (6mm) ribbon lengthwise around the bottle twice and secure it with a staple.

6 Tie a bow with the length of ⅝" (2cm) ribbon, and trim the ends with a V cut. Using the glue gun, glue the bow to the front of the bag. With craft glue, adhere the wax seal (see Making Polymer Clay Seals, page 116) to the center of the bow. The steps that follow are optional and include the addition of a tassel.

7 To add more elegance to your presentation, you can add a gold tassel under the gold seal. To create a knotted tassel, first wrap the gold embroidery floss around the 4½" (11cm) square piece of matboard, at least four times.

8 Tie the two ends of the gold cord together to make one large loop. This will serve as the tassel's suspension cord.

9 Take the wrapped floss off of the board and lay one end of the floss loops over the unknotted end of the suspension cord.

10 Pull the knotted end of the cord through where the floss and cord overlap. Pull the cord snug to secure the floss strands. Trim the floss at the opposite end to complete the tassel.

11 Glue the tassel to the front of the bag with the glue gun. Glue the bow from step 5 on top of that with the glue gun. With craft glue, adhere the wax seal (see Making Polymer Clay Seals, page 116) to the center of the bow.

CHOOSING
WINE
FOR YOUR WEDDING

Deciding on the right wine for your wedding can be fun, especially when you throw a wine-tasting party! Invite the bridesmaids and groomsmen to a casual evening of sampling several choices. Pick a few red, white and sparkling wines that are in your targeted price range and wrap each bottle in a brown paper bag. Affix a number to each for guests to refer to. You'll know what selections are the winners because they will be the first bottles to be emptied!

To determine the amount of wine that you will need for your wedding, a safe guideline is one-half bottle per person.

Please join us
for the
Dinner Reception
immediately
following
the ceremony
at
Park Shore Country Club
2415 Texas Avenue South
Saint Louis Park

the magic of a SNOWFALL

If you have always dreamt of a magical winter wedding, prepare to enchant your guests with a shimmering snowflake theme. This wonderful wintry set captures the romance of the season's first snowfall. With sparkling blues, whites and silvers, the palette may be icy and cool, but the excitement of the wedding day will cast a warm glow on the celebration!

A simple snowflake can create a sentimental and romantic feeling. These projects whisper a bit of magic with metallic inks, glitter and iridescent papers that glisten like snow. This set can complement an evening wedding, especially one with the majestic ambience of a winter ball.

From the invitation to the thank-you card, these frosty papercrafts are sure to melt the hearts of all your guests. The table ornaments and favor boxes are festive details that make the celebration especially memorable. Watching a snowfall will certainly rekindle fond memories of your wedding in the minds and hearts of all your friends and family!

INVITATION • THANK-YOU CARD • SNOWFLAKE DECORATION • CORNUCOPIA FAVOR

INVITATION

*Layers of iridescent paper give this invitation a soft shine, while the snowflake motif
sets a sentimental mood. One look at the invitation and your guests will be convinced
that winter is the most romantic time of the year—the perfect season for a wedding!*

what you will need

- 28" × 30" (71cm × 76cm) white iridescent cardstock
- 8½" × 11" (22cm × 28cm) blue metallic cardstock, 2 sheets
- 8½" × 11" (22cm × 28cm) snowflake translucent paper, 3 sheets
- A-7 envelope
- no. 4 envelope
- ten ⅛" (3mm) silver eyelets
- large silver snowflake sticker
- small silver snowflake sticker
- 24" (61cm) of ½" (1cm) blue iridescent ribbon
- blue metallic ink pad
- snowflake rubber stamp (PSX)
- scissors
- ruler
- pencil
- bone folder
- ⅛" (3mm) hole punch
- eyelet setter
- hammer
- cutting mat
- craft knife
- heat gun (optional)
- double-sided tape

Love is sacred and eternal
growing in strength and beauty.
We,
Karen Lillian Peterson
and
William Tyler Douglas
will exchange vows of dedication
to each other and God
on Saturday, the second of January
two thousand and two
at two o'clock in the afternoon
– at Park Assembly Church
1615 Texas Avenue South
Saint Louis Park, Minnesota

Please join us
for the
Dinner Reception
immediately
following
the ceremony
at
Park Shore Country Club
2415 Texas Avenue South
Saint Louis Park

We look forward
to celebrating with you!
Please reply by December 20, 2002
Name _____
_____ accept with pleasure
_____ decline with regret

1 Cut a 7" × 15" (18cm × 38cm) piece from the iridescent paper. With a ruler and a bone folder, fold the cut piece in half to 7" × 7½" (18cm × 19cm). Open the paper flat, and measure and mark 5" (13cm) to the left of the fold. With a ruler and bone folder, score and fold the left flap in toward the centerline. Repeat on the right side.

2 Open the card flat on the cutting mat. Place a ruler on the left fold. Make sure that the edge of the ruler is placed right on the fold line, then use the craft knife to cut a slit 3" (8cm) from the top of the card and ¾" (2cm) long. Repeat this on the right fold.

3 Cut one sheet of translucent paper to 4" × 6" (10cm × 15cm), and cut the metallic cardstock to a 2½" (6cm) square. Cut a piece of the iridescent cardstock to a 2" (5cm) square.

4 Using double-sided tape, center the 2" (5cm) iridescent square on the 2½" (6cm) metallic square. Place the large snowflake sticker in the center of the iridescent square.

5 Position the metallic square on the piece of translucent paper from step 3, and adhere it with double-sided tape.

6 Punch an ⅛" (3mm) hole in each corner of the translucent paper. Using the holes in the translucent paper as a template, punch holes through the four corners of the front panel of the iridescent invitation. Take care not to punch through the two flaps. Place eyelets in each of the holes and set them (see Setting Eyelets, page 118).

7 With the card laying flat, pull one end of the ribbon through the left-hand slit from the outside of the card to the inside. Continue pulling the ribbon through the slit on the right from the inside of the card to the outside. Pull

the ribbon through until both ends are the same length. Make sure the ribbon is flat.

8 Create a document for a finished size of 4" × 6" (10cm × 15cm). Start the wording ⅜" (1cm) from the top and center the text. Here the Freestyle Script font was used at 24pt. Print the invitation on a sheet of translucent paper, and trim to size.

9 Cut a 4¼" × 6¼" (11cm × 16cm) piece of iridescent cardstock and a 4¾" × 6¾" (12cm × 17cm) piece of metallic cardstock. Center the iridescent piece on the metallic piece and adhere it with double-sided tape.

10 Punch holes an ⅛" (3mm) in from the sides in the corners of the printed translucent paper. Place the printed translucent paper in the center of the iridescent piece from step 9. Using the translucent paper as a template, punch holes in the layered card. Put the eyelets in the holes and set them.

11 Create a document for a finished size of 3" × 5" (8cm × 13cm). Center the text, starting the words ⅝" (2cm) from the top. The font and its size are the same as in step 8. Print the reception card on translucent paper and trim to size.

12 Cut a piece of iridescent cardstock to 3¼" × 5¼" (8cm × 13cm). Cut the metallic cardstock to 4" × 6" (10cm × 15cm). Using double-sided tape, layer the two pieces together.

13 Place the printed reception card in the center of the layered card. Punch a hole ¾" (2cm) from the top in the center of the card. Put an eyelet in the hole and set it. Measure ¾" (2cm) from the bottom, and punch a hole in the center of the card. Place an eyelet in the hole and set it.

14 Create a document for a card that is 5" × 3½" (13cm × 9cm). Begin the text 1¼" (3cm) from the top, and center the text. Here the same font was used at 14pt. Print the response card on the iridescent cardstock, and trim to size.

15 Place the small snowflake sticker onto the response card, centering it between the top and the wording.

16 If you wish, stamp your envelopes to continue the theme of the invitations. The invitation fits in an A-7 envelope; the response card in a no. 4. Place scrap paper on your work area, and stamp each envelope with the snowflake stamp and blue ink. Let the design of the stamp go off the envelope edges. If you use a shiny paper, limit the amount of stamping you do as the ink smears easily. Allow sufficient time to dry (it may need to dry overnight) or try setting the ink with a heat gun.

17 To assemble the invitation pieces, place the invitation on the left side of the inside of the card from step 7, over the ribbon but under the flap. Put the response card under the flap of the small envelope and then on the right side, over the ribbon and under the flap. Place the reception card on top of the response card. Close the card and tie a bow with the two ends of the ribbon. Trim the ends of the ribbon.

THANK-YOU CARD

The thank-you card is the last wedding-related item that your guests will receive from you, so why not make it something memorable? Repeat the shimmering snowflake motif one final time by using it to decorate your thank-you card.

what you will **need**

- 8½" × 11" (22cm × 28cm) white iridescent cardstock
- 8½" × 11"" (22cm × 28cm) blue metallic cardstock, 2 sheets
- A-2 envelope
- glitter glue
- blue metallic ink pad
- snowflake rubber stamp (PSX)
- ruler
- scissors
- pencil
- bone folder
- double-sided tape
- heat gun (optional)

1 Cut the iridescent cardstock to 5½" × 8½" (14cm × 22cm). Randomly stamp the cut piece with the snowflake rubber stamp and blue ink. Let some of the stamps to go off the edge of the paper. Allow sufficient time for the ink to dry (possibly overnight), or set the ink with a heat gun. After the ink is dry, score and fold the piece in half to 4¼" × 5½" (11cm × 14cm). This card fits in a size A-2 envelope. If you like, stamp a random design on the envelope as well, using the same technique.

2 Cut a 2½" (6cm) square from the metallic cardstock and a 2" (5cm) square from the iridescent paper.

3 Ink one of the large snowflakes on the rubber stamp and center it on the iridescent square. Let the ink dry.

4 Put small drops of glitter glue in the center and on the tips of the snowflake. Follow the manufacturer's directions for the recommended drying time.

5 Center the stamped square onto the blue metallic square, and adhere them with double-sided tape. Center the layered piece on the front of the card, and adhere it with double-sided tape.

TIP

Shiny, coated paper has a nonporous surface. This means ink needs a longer drying time than that for porous or regular paper. Several hours — and plenty of space to spread the pieces out — are often needed. A heat gun may help to speed the process a bit. If you don't have that kind of time, substitute a more porous paper that can be just as elegant.

SNOWFLAKE DECORATION

Nothing captures the essence of winter like snowflakes. Surrounded by a blizzard of these frosty flakes, your guests will fall under the spell of wintry magic!

what you will need

- 8½" × 11" (22cm × 28cm) white iridescent vellum, 2 sheets
- scissors
- ruler
- pencil
- decorative hand punches
- decorative corner scissors
- glue stick
- fishing line

1 Trim the vellum to five 3¾" (10cm) square pieces. Fold each square in half diagonally.

2 Use the hand punches to cut shapes in one folded square, through both layers of paper. Make some holes directly on the fold.

3 Using the punched piece as a template, punch holes in the remaining four vellum squares. Unfold all of the pieces, and turn them over so that the diagonal fold points up. Fold each piece in half parallel to one side, unfold, and then fold in half perpendicular to the prior fold. There should now be four quadrants and one diagonal line on each of the five squares.

4 With one piece, push the two diagonal folds into the center, leaving a square on the top and on the bottom. With the two points of the inner folds facing up, use the corner scissors to cut through the four layers of vellum on the left side and on the right. Repeat for the other four pieces.

5 Using the glue stick, begin adhering the pieces together, lining up and attaching one flat side of one piece to the flat side of another. When complete, this should form a five-pointed, three-dimensional snowflake. Using a hand punch, punch a hole at the top of one of the layers that are glued together. Tie fishing line to this hole to hang the decoration.

CORNUCOPIA FAVOR

*A perfect accent to the snowflake theme, this icicle-shaped favor box is as much
a showpiece to accompany table settings as it is a container to hold goodies.
Fill the box with sweet treats to leave your guests feeling warm on the inside.*

what you will **need**

- 8½" × 11" (22cm × 28cm) light blue cardstock
- 8½" × 11" (22cm × 28cm) white cardstock
- 3½" × 6" (6cm × 15cm) cellophane bag
- snowflake sequins
- 12" (30cm) of ⅝" (2cm) wide sheer white ribbon
- decorative-edge scissors
- scissors
- ruler
- pencil
- bone folder
- pearl white acrylic paint
- snowflake stencil
- stencil sponge or cosmetic sponge
- foam plate
- paper towels
- double-sided tape
- white craft glue
- cornucopia pattern (on page 122)

1 Pour a small puddle of paint onto the foam plate. Cut a pile of paper towels into quarter sheets. With a cosmetic sponge, pick up some paint, dab it on the pile of paper towels to remove the excess, and work the paint up into the sponge.

2 Place the stencil on top of the blue cardstock, and apply the paint through the stencil with an up-and-down dabbing motion. Hold the stencil firmly to prevent it from slipping. If the paint seeps in under the stencil, you are using too much paint. Remember to wipe the sponge on the paper towels each time you reload the sponge. Fill the blue cardstock with snowflakes. Let dry completely.

3 Make a template for the box using the pattern and white cardstock. Trace the template onto the stenciled blue cardstock and cut out the cornucopia. Use the decorative-edge scissors to trim the top flaps. Score and fold the dashed lines with the bone folder. Assemble the box, using double-sided tape to adhere the flap to the outside of the box.

4 Place the favors inside the cellophane bag, and place the bag inside the box. Tie sheer white ribbon into a shoestring bow (see Shoestring Bow, page 120) around the top of the bag to close it. Glue a single snowflake sequin in the middle of the bow to finish the favor.

TIP

Stenciling is a quick and easy method for repeating a pattern on paper. Many beautiful motifs suitable for all wedding themes are available in ready-made stencils.

USING DECORATIVE
EDGE
SCISSORS

Decorative-edge scissors are a must when papercrafting. They are available in a wide range of different edges and give a professional touch to your projects. When cutting a long line with decorative-edge scissors, you need to line up the blade motifs. Make your first cut without cutting all the way to the end of the scissors. For the second cut, line up the motif like a puzzle, then continue cutting. When making a cut on a curve, make short cuts so that you cut just one or two motifs at a time.

PAPER TIPS
FOR STAMPING AND PRINTING

If you plan to rubber-stamp your invitation or print it on your computer's printer, pay special attention to the surface and finish of the paper you select. Take time to experiment with the paper and the technique you've chosen before purchasing paper for all your invitations.

Cardstock and text paper:
For rubber stamping, pick a smooth-surfaced paper with little texture. For printing, a smooth, more matte finish often works best. However, some more textured paper works best for some ink-jet printers.

Glossy and translucent papers:
For stamping, emboss the ink with heat to make it permanent. You can check your local craft or stamp store for special inks that will dry on vellum without being heat embossed. For printing, experiment with both sides of the translucent paper or change the settings on your printer to "transparency." If printing on this paper doesn't work, try using a photocopier.

Handmade papers:
These papers can be more absorbent, which will alter the results you get with stamping, hand printing or computer printing. Experiment with different paper choices before making final decisions. Some papers can be trimmed to size and run through an ink-jet printer.

MATERIALS

In choosing to create your wedding papercrafts, you have found a unique way to personalize your special day. The projects and ideas in this book cover a variety of skill levels and time commitments, as well as a wide range of styles. Before you select the projects that you'll make for your wedding, consider the following four questions to help you narrow your choices for invitations and accessories:

PAPER

The paper you choose for your wedding projects can function as an integral part of your design or simply as a foundation upon which you build your design. Base your selection of paper on what is most suitable for your project. With the wide assortment of paper available, you are sure to find something that is as beautiful as it is suitable!

Card or cover stock: Cardstock, often referred to as cover stock or 65-80 pound (140gsm to 170gsm) cardstock, is a heavier-weight paper. It is available in many colors, patterns, textures and finishes, ranging from smooth to heavily textured and matte to glossy. Cardstock works well as a substantial base for an invitation.

Text paper: Text-weight paper is a medium-weight paper. It is available in many colors, patterns, textures and finishes. Stationery paper and scrapbook paper offer many choices in this type of paper. Computer paper is also text-weight. Because text-weight paper is weaker and less substantial than cardstock, its uses are more limited. For invitations, text-weight paper would work better layered onto a piece of cardstock. It would also work well for making envelopes (see Making Envelopes, page 112).

Specialty paper: "Specialty paper" describes a wide variety of paper, including marbleized, suede, metallic, corrugated, tissue and wrapping paper, as well as handmade paper that has flowers, seeds, leaves and other objects embedded in it.

The weight, texture and surface finish vary considerably from paper to paper. Thicker, more substantial specialty paper can be used like cardstock, and medium-weight paper can be used like text-weight paper. Very thin specialty paper, which appears almost transparent, can be used to wrap or layer onto invitations.

Because specialty paper is often made by hand, not machines, it is not uncommon for the paper to lack a grain. Sheets come in a variety of sizes, ranging from very large to the standard 8½" × 11" (22cm × 28cm).

Translucent paper: Translucent paper, often called vellum, is characterized by its see-through quality. It can be found in many colors and designs and is available in both text-weight and cardstock weight. Different sizes of envelopes are also made of translucent paper. The use of translucent papers for wedding invitations is very popular, as these papers lend a very elegant and modern touch.

Text-weight vellum works well as an overlay on patterned papers. You can print text on a piece of vellum and then secure it on top of cardstock. Any pattern or design on the cardstock would be visible, though muted, through the vellum without interfering with the legibility of the printed text. Texture on the cardstock may not show.

Various types of handmade paper can add rich texture to your papercrafts.

All machine-made paper has a grain direction. This means that the paper fibers all lie in one direction. Folds made with the grain (parallel to the fibers) are stronger and crisper than those made against the grain. To determine the grain, curl your paper one direction then the other. You'll feel less resistance when bending the paper with the grain.

Using adhesives on translucent papers is a challenge; because you can see through the paper, you often can see the adhesive being used. Vellum can be attached to other paper with ribbon, eyelets, brads, clips, wax seals, photo corners and special double-sided tape (see Adhesives, page 109).

FOLDING TOOLS

One key to well-made papercrafts is crisp, straight folds. The easiest way to get a crisp fold is to score the paper first. A score is a halfcut that breaks through, or condenses, the top fibers of the paper, and it is made on what will be the outside of the fold. Following are a number of tools you may use to create a score.

Bone folder: This flat piece of smooth bone is usually rounded at one end and pointed at the other. For each fold, draw the bone folder along a ruler edge toward you, pressing down to score a fold line. Fold along this line and use the bone folder to firmly reinforce each fold by smoothing the fold down sharply.

Stylus: You can also use a pressure embossing stylus rather than the bone folder. Run the stylus along the edge of a ruler on a slightly padded surface, such as a cutting mat, to score the paper for folding.

Slide cutter: The slide cutter also can be used to score straight lines. Replace the cutting blade with the black scoring blade to score fold lines.

THE SCIENCE OF
GLUE

Most glue is water based, but some glues have a higher water content than others. This is a very important factor when you adhere paper, as glue with a higher water content can cause your paper to wrinkle or buckle. Glues like those made for scrapbooking are formulated to have a high solid content and therefore do not create wrinkles or waves when adhering papers together. Check labels for suggested uses. If you use glue with a higher water content to secure two or more sheets of papers together, weigh down your paper with books or some other flat, smooth, heavy object to press out the wrinkles during the drying process.

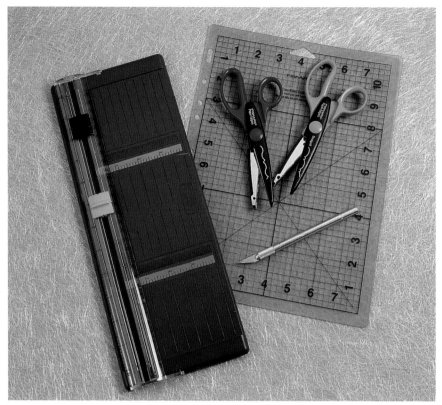

A slide cutter, decorative scissors, craft knife and cutting mat are all tools to have on hand.

CUTTING TOOLS

To help the creation of your papercrafts go smoothly, keep sharp, quality cutting tools available. You may need a few different tools to make quick work of the cutting. Following are a few you may want to have on hand.

Handheld scissors: A large, sharp pair is useful for cutting down large sheets of paper, while a small, sharp pair of craft scissors is good for cutting out small pieces and images or for cutting embellishments, like ribbon. For precise cutting of small paper pieces, move the paper and keep the scissors stationary as you cut.

Craft knife, metal ruler and self-healing cutting mat: A scalpel-type craft knife with a replaceable pointed blade is essential. It is an all-purpose knife for cutting all the different types of papers. Scissors don't give you the straight, sharp edges you get with a craft knife. Make sure you have a supply of additional blades to ensure you'll always have a sharp cutting edge. To protect your work surface, use a self-healing cutting mat when using a craft knife. A 12" (30cm) straight-edge metal ruler with cork backing works well as a nonslip guide for your straight cuts.

Slide cutter: A sliding-blade paper trimmer is useful for general cuts. A paper trimmer makes the job much easier and faster than a craft knife for straight-line trimming. To use, line up the paper so the top edge is flush against the ridge at the top of the cutter. Slide the blade down to cut. When cutting larger sheets of paper, swing out the marker arm on the left underside of the cutter. You can cut up to five sheets of light-weight paper at a time.

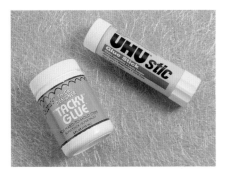

Craft glue and a glue stick are must-haves.

A large variety of embellishments and decorative materials are available to give your papercrafts a unique look.

ADHESIVES

After you spend time and effort creating your wedding papercrafts, you'll want them to stay together. There are many different adhesives available, each with an ideal use. Following are some adhesives that you may want to have on hand.

Glue stick: Glue that comes in a stick form for paper is convenient and simple to use. Use the large glue sticks that are nontoxic and acid free for laminating papers together, for gluing paper panels onto cards and for basic papercrafting. Use a "glue sheet" (such as wax paper) to protect your work surface. Apply the glue evenly from the center of the paper to the edges and burnish the pieces firmly with the side of the bone folder. Applying too much glue may cause the paper to warp. For gluing pieces with cut-out details (such as a strip punched with a border punch), place the piece on a glue sheet and use an up-and-down dabbing motion to apply the glue. This prevents excess glue from building up in the cut areas and smudging your surface.

White craft glue: White craft glue is used when applying heavier paper panels and embellishments. Use a disposable glue brush to apply a thin, even coating of glue to the paper; work from the center of the paper to the edges. A glue sheet under the piece can help to prevent glue from getting on the top of the piece. Acrylic découpage finish, or thin white glue, is used for découpage projects. This glue will seep through the finer handmade papers.

Double-sided tape: This tape is great for adhering and layering text-weight or other light-weight paper. It works best on smooth papers that aren't highly textured or very fibrous. Most double-sided tapes have a middle layer of cellophane with adhesive on both sides of it. Some varieties are about an ⅛" (3mm) wide and come in a refillable applicator. There is even a double-sided tape that is made specifically for translucent papers.

Spray adhesives: Spray adhesives produce a fine sticky mist that is perfect for use on thin or delicate papers, handmade paper and light-weight fabrics. If the paper is very thin, the top of the paper might feel tacky after it is adhered. One advantage of using a spray adhesive is that it does not dry quickly and it therefore allows repositioning. It also works well for adhering translucent pieces to paper, as it is not very visible.

Use caution with spray adhesives. Place papers inside a large cardboard box and spray them there to prevent the overspray from falling onto the surrounding work area. Use the spray sparingly and in a well-ventilated area.

EMBELLISHMENTS

Ribbon, fibers, charms and wax seals are just a few of the wonderful embellishments that can make your papercrafts truly unique.

Some, like charms, are simply decorative. You can string them onto ribbon or fibers to attach them to your crafts, or you can glue them in place with craft glue.

Other embellishments, like ribbon, eyelets, brads, clips, wax seals and stickers, are not only beautiful but can be functional too. Instead of gluing two layers of paper together, try securing them with eyelets or brads. Close a party favor with a clip or wrap it with ribbon. Gather different embellishments and play with them to see what works best for your papercrafts.

TECHNIQUES

The following pages show you some techniques necessary to truly personalize your wedding papercrafts. Combining two or more of these methods creates a unique look that brings together the colors, symbols and overall theme of your wedding.

PRINTING ON YOUR COMPUTER

Your home computer can be a wonderful tool when you create your wedding papercrafts. It can allow you to design and print your own invitations, response cards, menu cards, thank-you cards and so much more. There are so many fonts on your computer or available to download off the Internet that creating a look for your wedding is easy. Your theme, whether elegant and formal or casual and whimsical, can be easily conveyed by the font you choose for all your papercrafts.

To maximize the yield from the least amount of paper, set up your documents so that you can print multiple cards on one piece of paper. At the right is how I set up a document on my computer to print out 2¾" × 3¼" (7cm × 8cm) pieces on a sheet of 8½" × 11" (22cm × 28cm) paper. Creating columns in a document allows you to evenly space the pieces and get the most pieces on each page. By shading the column lines a light gray, you will have cutting guides printed on every page; your pieces will be uniform, and the cutting will go quickly. Cutting straight lines, like those for the cards shown here, goes quickly with a slide cutter (see Cutting Tools, page 107).

Before you purchase all the paper for your invitations, print a sample piece to be sure the paper feeds through your printer and the ink adheres to the paper. Vellum, cardstock, some handmade papers, text-weight and decorative papers can usually be used with an ink-jet printer.

The final step before printing your papercrafts is to carefully read the wording. Do not rely on the spell checker; proofread your information for accuracy, and double-check the spelling of all names.

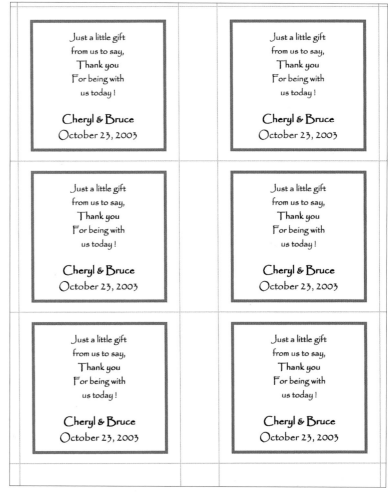

These small cards can be used as thank-you notes inside a favor pouch. To print them on your computer, create a document with columns to maximize the space you have on the large sheet of paper. Here, six 2¾" × 3¼" (7cm × 8cm) cards are on an 8½" × 11" (22cm × 28cm) sheet.

MAKING AND USING TEMPLATES

When you need to create multiples of any papercraft, it helps to make a template from heavy paper that you can easily reuse. If you are making an invitation that requires holes to be punched for eyelets, you could make a template with the holes placed in the correct spots; you wouldn't need to measure their placement on each invitation. Your template could be more complex if it's for an intricate favor box.

To make your own template for holes on an invitation or booklet, cut a piece of heavy cardstock to the size of the invitation or booklet. Measure and mark the placement of the holes, then punch holes at the marks. When making the items, align the paper with the template and punch holes using the template as a guide.

To make a template from a pattern, trace or photocopy the pattern. When tracing, make the cutting lines solid and the folding lines dashed. Glue the copy onto a heavy piece of cardstock with a glue stick. For an even stronger template, you could laminate the top with a self-adhesive plastic sheet. Using a cutting mat, ruler and craft knife for straight edges and scissors for curved edges, cut out the template.

To use a template for cutting and folding, follow these easy steps.

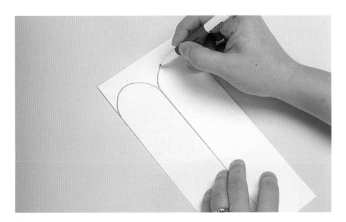

1 Trace Around Template
With a little piece of low-tack tape, tape the template down to the paper. Trace around the template with an air-erase pen or a light pencil.

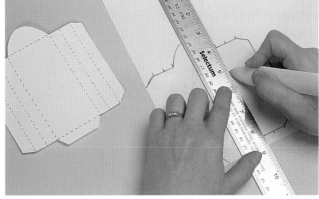

2 Score Paper
Mark the score lines indicated with a dotted line. Remove the template and score the paper with a bone folder and ruler where indicated, lining up the marks on the paper.

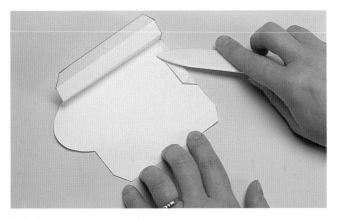

3 Cut Paper and Assemble
Cut out the pieces. Fold and burnish all the scored lines with a bone folder. Glue the flaps to form the container. It is generally best to glue down the longer edges first.

TIP

When tracing a template onto paper, try using an air-erase pen. These pens make marks that disappear in twelve to twenty-four hours. Before you begin making templates with this type of pen, test it on your paper to make sure it will disappear completely. You can find air-erase pens in quilting and fabric stores.

MAKING ENVELOPES

Matching your envelopes to your invitations is sometimes easier if you make them yourself! You can find templates for envelopes of all sizes at craft and stamp stores.

1 Trace Envelope

To make a pattern, carefully take apart an envelope that is the size and shape you like. Trace this pattern onto the back of your paper. Also mark where the folds will be.

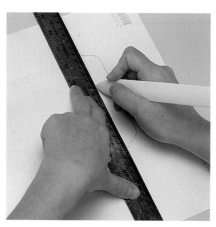

2 Score Fold Lines

Score along the lines to be folded with a ruler and a bone folder.

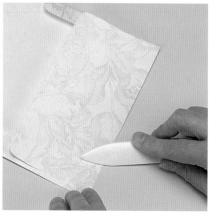

3 Cut Out the Envelope and Fold

Cut out the envelope using a ruler and craft knife for the straight lines and scissors for the rounded edges. Fold the sides of the envelope, and burnish the folds with the bone folder.

4 Glue Side Flaps Closed

Using a glue stick, glue down the side flaps to form the envelope. To seal, use a glue stick to glue the top flap down.

TIP

To cut down on tracing, use the computer to create the envelope outline. Print this onto your chosen paper using a very pale ink color.

LINING ENVELOPES

This is a simple and quick method to line plain envelopes with decorative paper to match your handmade invitation. Use wrapping paper or text-weight decorative paper. This method works for all sizes and types of envelopes.

1 Cut Decorative Paper to Fit
Cut the decorative paper to the width of the envelope's interior (1/8" [3mm] smaller than the envelope's outside width) and to the height with the flap up.

2 Trim Around Flap
Slip the decorative paper into the envelope. Turn over the envelope and using scissors, trim the decorative piece even with the shape of the flap.

3 Trim to Expose Adhesive Strip
Remove the decorative paper from the envelope. Measure the width of the glue strip on the envelope; in this case it's 3/8" (1cm). Trim that amount from the bottom edge of the decorative paper.

4 Glue Liner in Place
Using a glue stick, place glue along the wrong side of the top of the flap of the decorative lining. Insert the lining into the envelope, and push it all the way to the bottom. Burnish the lining to the envelope with the bone folder.

5 Score at Fold
Fold the flap down and burnish it with the bone folder. Your perfectly lined envelope is ready to use.

MAKING A QUICK BOX

This is a very quick technique for making a lidded box. It requires two pieces of cardstock both cut to the same size. You can use any rectangular or square dimensions for your box. Cardstock can be used for boxes up to 6" (15cm) wide. For larger boxes, a heavier paper or a cardstock laminated with decorative paper should be used. You can also laminate a light-weight decorative paper to cardstock for an attractive box lining.

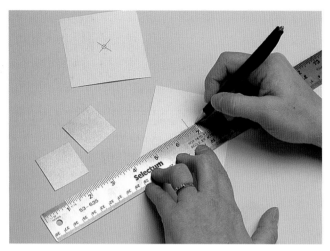

1 Trim Papers and Create Template

For a finished box measuring 1¾" × 1¾" × ¾" (45mm × 45mm × 19mm), cut two squares measuring 3¼" × 3¼" (83mm × 83mm). Cut two squares measuring 1½" × 1½" (38mm × 38mm) to line the inside of the box. Working with the larger square pieces, cross mark the center on both pieces. On the piece of paper that will be the box top, make a ¼" (6mm) circle around the center mark. (Make a simple template by punching a ¼" [6mm] hole in a piece of scrap. It doesn't matter what size box you make; the circle size is always the same.)

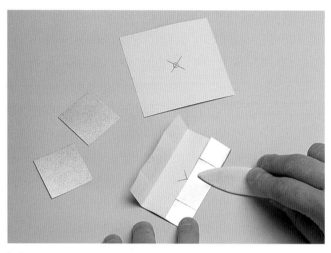

2 Fold Box Bottom Sides

To make the bottom of the box, fold each side of the square to the center cross mark, and burnish every fold with a bone folder.

3 Fold Box Top Sides

For the box top, fold each side to the outside of the small circle and burnish every fold with a bone folder. This makes the box top slightly larger than the box bottom for a perfect fit.

4 Trim Corners

Trim a triangle out of each corner on both the box bottom and top.

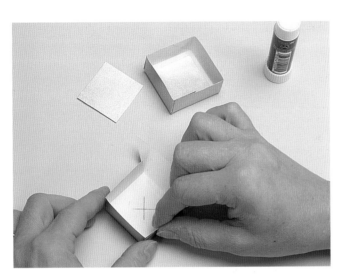

5 Glue Flaps in Place

Place glue on the triangle flaps of the box with the glue stick and fold up the sides, tucking the flaps inside the box. Apply glue to the back of one small square and place it in the bottom of the box. Repeat for the lid.

RECTANGULAR
BOXES

To create a box that is rectangular, rather than square, fold the long sides in to meet the center cross mark, and check the measurement of the distance from the paper edge to the fold. Then, rather than fold the short sides in to the center, fold them in on a line at this same measurement.

BOX SIZES

Start With Paper This Size	To Make a Box of This Size
2" × 3" (51mm × 76mm)	1" × 2" × 1/2" (25mm × 51mm × 13mm)
3" × 3" (76mm × 76mm)	1 1/2" × 1 1/2" × 3/4" (38mm × 28mm × 19mm)
3" × 4" (76mm × 102mm)	1 1/2" × 2 1/2" × 3/4" (38mm × 64mm × 19mm)
4" × 4" (102mm × 102mm)	2" × 2" × 1" (51mm × 51mm × 25mm)
4" × 5" (102mm × 127mm)	2" × 3" × 1" (51mm × 76mm × 25mm)
5" × 5" (127mm × 127mm)	2 1/2" × 2 1/2" × 1 1/4" (64mm × 64mm × 32mm)
5" × 6" (127mm × 152mm)	2 1/2" × 3 1/2" × 1 1/4" (64mm × 89mm × 32mm)
6" × 6" (152mm × 152mm)	3" × 3" × 1 1/2" (76mm × 76mm × 38mm)

MAKING WAX SEALS

Wax seals, especially when stamped with a special rubber stamp or metal seal, lend an elegant look to any wedding papercrafts. Traditional wax seals are made from a blend of wax and shellac that creates a very hard seal. When making a seal, it is normal to have soot in the melted wax. This creates a nice marbled effect with the colored wax. You can control the amount of soot by changing the angle of the sealing wax stick.

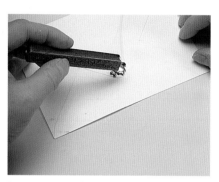

1 Melt the Wax

Light the wick of the wax stick with a match or lighter. Allow the wax to drip onto the paper in a 1"-diameter (3cm) ring, then fill the ring with drips of wax.

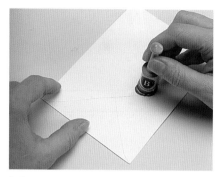

2 Press the Seal into the Wax

Blow out the flame. Immediately press the image into the hot wax, and hold it for about five seconds. Work quickly or the wax will harden before you can impress the seal.

3 Remove the Seal

Remove the seal or stamp to reveal the finished wax seal.

MAKING POLYMER CLAY SEALS

A stronger and more uniform alternative to a wax seal is a seal made from polymer clay. These seals are especially nice as permanent accents on papercrafts. You can make about two dozen 1"-diameter (3cm) seals from a 2-ounce (57g) package of polymer clay. When making the seals, use a glazed tile as the work surface and baking surface.

1 Stamp the Image into the Seal

Knead the clay to make it soft and pliable. Form the clay into ⅝"-diameter (2cm) balls. Flatten each ball into a 1"-diameter (3cm) disc, and impress the design with a stamp.

2 Highlight and Bake

Highlight the seals with metallic mica powder. Bake the seals to harden in a 275°F (135°C) oven for thirty minutes.

MAKING TASSELS

Tassels add texture and sophistication to your invitation elements or reception decorations, and they are easy to create. A multitude of fibers are available at your local needlepoint shops and craft stores.

1 Create Suspension Cord
Wrap floss or decorative fibers around a piece of cardboard that is ½" (1cm) longer than the desired tassel length. Wind an amount that appears on one side of the cardboard to be half of the desired fullness. Carefully slide the bulk of fibers off of the cardboard. One end will serve as the top and be tied off. Make a suspension cord by cutting a 10" (25cm) cord and knotting the ends to form a loop. Loop-knot the suspension cord around the top of the tassel loops to hold.

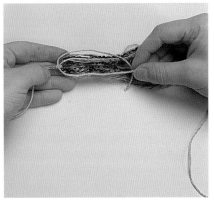

2 Cut a Piece of Binding Thread
Cut a 36" (91cm) piece of binding thread to wrap around the top of the tassel. Make a loop and place it on the tassel at the top with the long tail hanging down.

3 Begin Wrapping Binding Thread
Begin to wrap the binding thread firmly around the top of the tassel. Start at the bottom and wrap toward the top of the tassel.

4 Tie Off the Binding
Continue to neatly wrap the binding thread, and then thread the end through the loop made in step 2.

5 Pull Ends Through to Hide
Pull on the bottom of the loop to bury the wrapping end inside of the wrapped threads.

6 Trim Excess Threads
Trim off the excess length of each end of the binding thread. Cut through the bottom of the tassel threads and trim evenly.

SETTING EYELETS

Eyelets are attractive and functional embellishments for cards and papercrafts. Eyelets come in several sizes, the most popular being ⅛" (3mm). They also come in many colors and shapes. Use them to attach panels to cards or as decorative accents to your papercrafts.

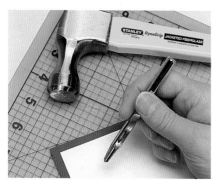  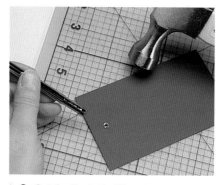

1 Create a Hole for the Eyelet

With a hole punch, make a hole where you want to set the eyelet.

2 Insert the Eyelet

Insert the eyelet into the hole and turn the paper back over.

3 Set the Eyelet in Place

Place the tip of the eyelet setter in the eyelet and tap the end with a hammer several times until the back of the eyelet is pressed flat.

CARVING STAMPS

If you can't find that perfect rubber stamp for your papercrafts, try making your own. Design an image or copy a design from a motif on your wedding dress, a flower you are using in your celebration or a symbolic motif with special meaning. Stamp patterns for some of the motifs in this book are on page 123.

1 Transfer the Image

Use a soft pencil to trace or draw the design onto a piece of tracing paper. Place the image face down onto the carving block. Rub the back of the paper with a pencil, transferring the image to the block. This will be a mirror image of the original.

2 Carve the Image

Lift the pattern off the block and make sure your whole design has been transferred successfully. Trim away the excess carving block with an art knife. With a fine cutter, outline the whole design. With a larger U-shaped cutter, carve away the parts of the block that should not be stamped.

3 Refine and Stamp the Image

Continue to carve until you are satisfied with the image. Do not worry about some of the cut area showing in the finished stamped print. This adds a hand-carved look that many stamp artists include in the finished design. Add ink, and stamp your new image.

THERMAL EMBOSSING

Thermal embossing is a technique used to raise a stamped image above the surface of the paper. Many embossing powders are available in many different colors and finishes—shiny, matte, glittery or iridescent. For this process you will need a rubber stamp, a pigment ink pad, embossing powder and a heat gun.

4 Stamp and Add Powder to the Image

Stamp the image onto your paper using a pigment ink stamp pad. Sprinkle on the embossing powder immediately while the ink is still wet, completely covering the image.

5 Tap Off Excess Powder

Tap the excess powder onto a sheet of scrap paper so you can reuse it for further embossing.

6 Brush the Surface

With a clean, dry brush, remove any specks of embossing powder that have stuck to the paper anywhere other than the image.

7 Melt the Powder

Funnel the excess powder back into the jar for later use. Using a heat gun, blow hot air onto the stamped image for a few seconds. You will be able to see the powder melt. Do not overdo it, or the image will be blurry.

SHOESTRING BOW

Bows are a finishing touch. Use them to embellish cards, favors or wrapped gifts. Bows are much simpler to make than you might think. The right ribbons and a little adjusting will guarantee you success every time. This is called a shoestring bow because it is tied just like your shoelace!

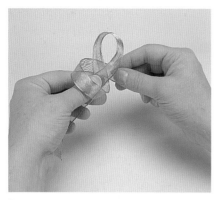

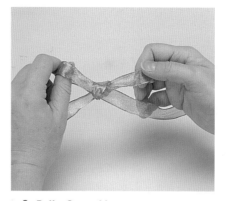

1 Form a Loop
Start the bow with the ribbon still on the roll. Form a loop, hold the bottom, and wrap the ribbon around to the back.

2 Pull a Second Loop
Pull another loop through the loop formed by the wrap, and pull to form the bow.

3 Adjust the Loops and Trim
Pull on the ends to size the loops. Cut the end from the roll of ribbon to the desired length, and then trim each end with an angle cut.

MULTI-LOOP BOW

This is a more elaborate-looking bow that works well for decorations as well as finishing wrapped gifts.

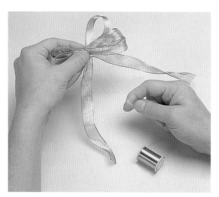

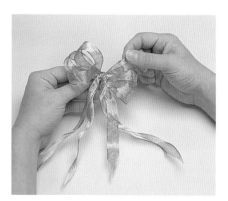

1 Form Loops
Start with the ribbon end pointing down and make loops of ribbon in a figure eight pattern. Keep all the loops the same size.

2 Wrap the Ribbon with Wire
Make as many loops as you like, finishing with an equal number of loops on each end and the tails pointing down. Trim the second tail to the same length as the first tail. Leaving a 3" (8cm) tail of wire, neatly and tightly wrap wire around the center.

3 Secure Wire and Adjust Loops
Twist the wire tightly and trim the wire so you have two 3" (8cm) lengths of wire at the back. Tie two pieces of ribbon to the center of the bow to form four tails. Trim the ends of the ribbon and fluff the loops to finish. Use the wire ends to attach the bow to your project.

TAILORED BOW

Though similar to the previous two bows, the tailored bow is slightly more formal and a bit more sleek.

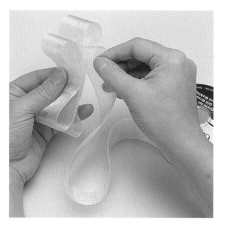

1 Create Four Loops

Looping the ribbon side to side, form four loops. Make the top loops slightly smaller than the bottom loops.

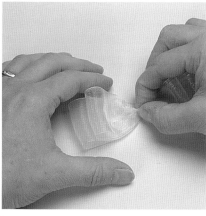

2 Pinch the Center

Trim the ribbon from the roll. Leave about 1" (3cm) of overlap in the center. Pinch the center of the bow with your fingers, and place the bow on a hard surface.

3 Secure With Wire

Leaving a 3" (8cm) tail, wrap thin wire neatly and tightly around the center. Wrap the wire about five times. Twist the wire and trim the wire tails.

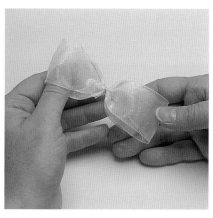

4 Adjust the Loops

Fluff the loops, and adjust them as desired, to form the bow.

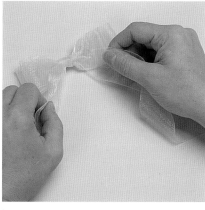

5 Tie On the Tails

To form the tails of the bow, tie a piece of ribbon around the center of the bow with a single knot. This also helps to hide the wire.

6 Trim and Embellish

Finish the tail ends with a V cut by folding the ribbon in half length-wise and cutting the end at an angle. Leave the bow as is, or embellish it with a charm or button in the center. You can add extra tails by knotting more ribbon lengths around the center.

TIP

Form your bows right from the roll to minimize waste and maximize the number of bows you'll get from each roll of ribbon.

PATTERNS

Heart Box and Table Confetti page, 20 and 21.
Enlarge at 114% to bring to full size.

Wrap, page 32. Enlarge first at 200%, then at 156% to bring to full size.

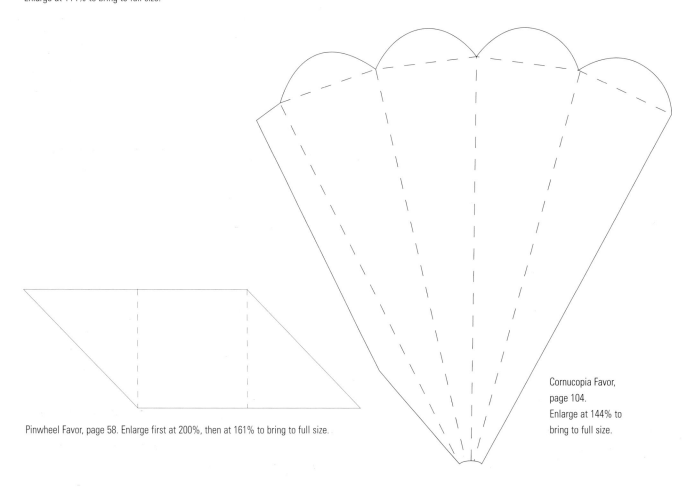

Pinwheel Favor, page 58. Enlarge first at 200%, then at 161% to bring to full size.

Cornucopia Favor,
page 104.
Enlarge at 144% to
bring to full size.

Leaf Table Confetti, page 77. Enlarge first at 200%, then at 116% to bring to full size.

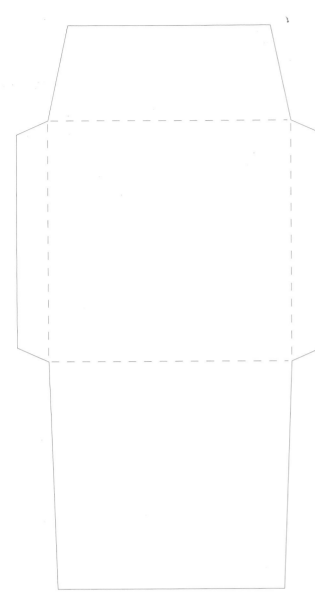

CD Holder, pages 34 and 66. Enlarge at 200% to bring to full size.

Carve Your Own Stamp

Fleur-de-lis, page 94.
Enlarge at 122% to bring to full size.

Carve Your Own Stamp

Daisy Table Confetti, page 49.
Enlarge at 120% to bring to full size.

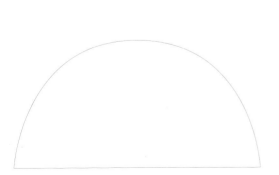

Flower Girl Basket, page 43. Enlarge first at 200%, then at another 200% to bring to full size.

Carve Your Own Stamp

Salmon Leaf motif,
pages 62–69.
Enlarge at 150% to bring to full size.

Carve Your Own Stamp

Leaf Accent, page 38.
Enlarge at 150% to bring to full size.

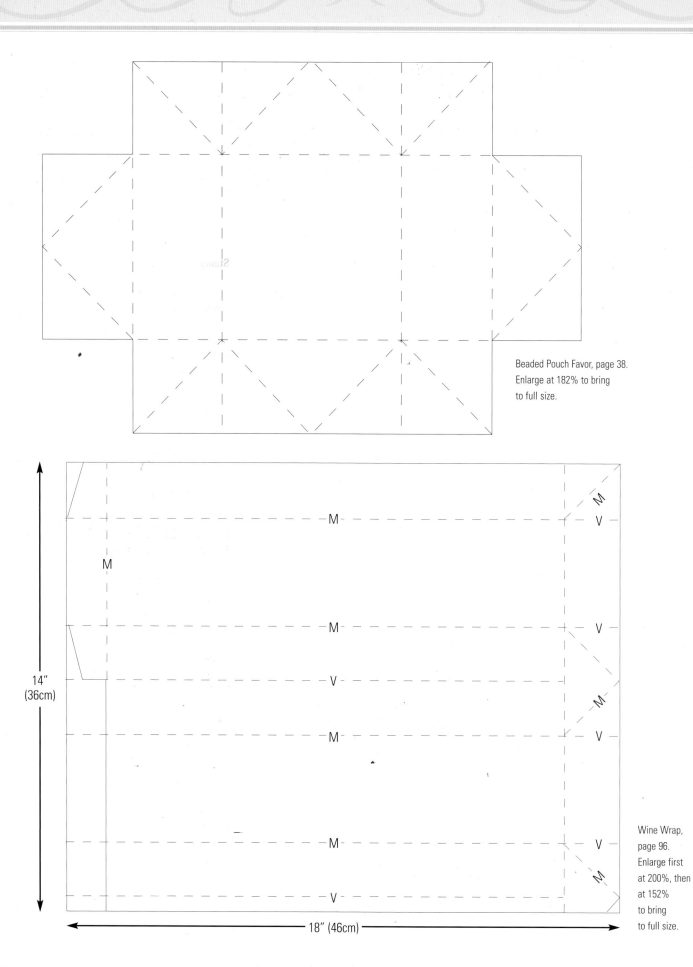

Beaded Pouch Favor, page 38.
Enlarge at 182% to bring
to full size.

M

M
M

M
V

M

V

M
M

V

14"
(36cm)

V

M
V

M

V

Wine Wrap,
page 96.
Enlarge first
at 200%, then
at 152%
to bring
to full size.

V

M

V

18" (46cm)

RESOURCES

Most of the materials and supplies used to make the projects in this book can be found at your local arts and crafts store, scrapbook or rubber stamping store, fabric store or office supply store. If you can't locate a particular item, contact the product manufacturer, using the information below; they should be able to help you find a retailer near you.

PAPER

Anna Griffin Incorporated
733 Lambert Drive
Atlanta, GA 30324
888-817-8170
www.annagriffin.com

EK Success
P.O. Box 1141
Clifton, NJ 07014-1141
800-524-1349
www.eksuccess.com

K&Company
8500 NW River Park Drive
Pillar no. 136
Parkville, MO 64152
888-244-2083
www.kandcompany.com

Papers by Catherine
11328 Southpost Oak Rt. Ste. 108
Houston, TX 77035
713-723-3334
www.papersbycatherine.com

Paper Adventures
901 S. Fifth Street
Milwaukee, WI 53204
414-645-5760
www.paperadventures.com

Savoir-Faire
40 Leveroni Court
Novato, CA 94949
415-884-8090
www.savoirfaire.com

What's New International
4811 East Julep
Suite 107
Mesa, AZ 85205
800-272-3874
www.scrap-ease.com

RUBBER STAMPS

Delta Technical Coatings
2550 Pellissier Place
Whittier, CA 90601-1505
800-423-4135
www.deltacrafts.com
(Rubber Stampede stamps)

Inkadinkado
61 Holton Street
Woburn, MA 01801
800-888-4652
www.inkadinkado.com

JudiKins
17803 South Harvard Boulevard
Gardena, CA 90248
310-515-1115
www.judikins.com

Magenta Art Stamps
2275 Bombardier
Sainte-Julie, Quebec J3E 2J9
450-922-5253
www.magentarubberstamps.com

Plaid Enterprises Inc.
3225 Westech Drive
Norcross, GA 30092
800-842-4197
www.plaidonline.com
(All Night Media brand stamps)

PSX (Personal Stamp Exchange)
360 Sutton Place
Santa Rosa, CA 95409
866-779-9877
www.psxdesign.com

Printworks
12342 McCann Drive
Santa Fe Springs, CA 90670
800-854-6558
www.printworkscollection.com

Stamp Francisco
308 SE 271st Court
Camas, WA 98607
360-210-4031
www.stampfrancisco.com

Stampa Rosa, Inc.
60 Maxwell Court
Santa Rosa, CA 95401
800-554-5755

Stampendous
1240 North Red Gum
Anaheim, CA 92806
800-869-0474
www.stampendous.com

EMBELLISHMENTS

Boutique Trims/Accent Factory
21200 Pontiac Trail
South Lyon, MI 48178
888-437-3888; 248-437-2017
www.boutiquetrims.com
(Jewelry charms)

Carlson Craft
P.O. Box 8700
Mankato, MN 56002-8700
800-545-4065
www.carlsoncraft.com
(Tassels)

C.M. Offray & Son, Inc.
Lion Ribbon
Route 24, Box 601
Chester, NJ 07930-0601
800-344-5533
www.offray.com
(Ribbon)

GENERAL SUPPLIES

Cavallini and Company, Inc.
1630 17th Street
San Francisco, CA 94107
800-226-5287
(Clipiola spiral clips)

Creative Impressions
2520 West Colorado Avenue
Colorado Springs, CO 80904
719-577-4858
www.creativeimpressions.com
(Eyelets, eyelet setters)

Making Memories
1168 West 500th North
Centerville, UT 84014
801-286-5263
www.makingmemories.com
(Eyelets, brads, and eyelet setters)

Marcel Schurman
500 Chadbourne Road
Box 6030
Fairfield, CA 94533
800-333-6724
www.schurman.com
(Felt leaf with beads)

Marvy Uchinda
3535 Del Amo Boulevard
Torrance, CA 90503
800-541-5877
www.uchida.com
(Punches)

Midori Ribbon
708 Sixth Avenue North
Seattle, WA 98109
800-659-3049
www.midoriribbon.com
(Ribbon)

Pressed Petals, Inc.
47 South Main Street
Richfield, UT 84701
800-748-4656
www.pressedpetals.com
(Dried and pressed flowers)

Raffit Ribbons
1150 Shames Drive
Westbury, NY 11590
516-333-6778
www.raffitribbons.com
(Synthetic raffia)

Beacon Adhesives
125 MacQuesten Pkwy South
Mt. Vernon, NY 10550
914-699-3400
www.beaconcreates.com
(Glues)

Books By Hand
P.O. Box 8819
Albuquerque, NM 87198
505-255-3534
www.booksbyhand.com
(Bone folder, awl, bookbinding supplies, and handmade papers)

Clearsnap
P.O. Box 98
Anacortee, WA 98221
800-448-4862
www.clearsnap.com
(Rubber stamping inks)

Duncan Enterprises
5673 E. Shields Avenue
Fresno, CA 93727
800-438-6226
www.duncancrafts.com
(Aleene's white craft glues)

Environmental Technologies
300 South Bay Depot Road
Fields Landing, CA 95537
707-443-9323
www.eti-usa.com
(Envirotex Lite)

Fiskars Brands, Inc.
7811 West Stewart Avenue
Wausau, WI 54401
800-500-4849
www.fiskars.com
(Scissors, decorative scissors, slide cutter and rotary cutters)

Jacquard Products
Rubert, Gibbon & Spider, Inc.
P.O. Box 425
Healdsburg, CA 95448
707-433-9577
www.jacquardproducts.com
(Pearl-Ex metallic powders)

3M Corporate Headquarters
3M Center
St. Paul, MN 55144
888-364-3577
www.mmm.com
(Double-sided tape, glue stick, spray adhesive)

Polyform Products Co.
1901 Estes Avenue
Elk Grove Village, IL 60007
847-427-0020
www.sculpey.com
(Premo! Sculpey polymer clay and tools)

Sakura of America
30780 San Clement St.
Hayward, CA 94544
510-475-8880
www.gellyroll.com
(Permanent markers)

Tombo
355 Satellite Boulevard
Suite 300
Suwanee, GA 30024
800-835-3232
www.tombowusa.com
(Markers)

INDEX

The best in wedding inspirations and creative crafts is from North Light Books!